TYPE 1 DIABETES KID-FRIENDLY COOKBOOK

The Super Easy Sugar-Free Recipe Book for
Diabetic Kids with Tips to Help Manage Blood
Sugar Levels and Fight Symptoms

Steve Bryant, MD, RD

Copyright Page

Table of Contents

Chapter 1: Introduction

Type 1 diabetes, once known as juvenile diabetes or insulin-dependent diabetes, is a chronic condition. In this condition, the pancreas makes little or no insulin. It's estimated that about 1.25 million Americans live with it.

When you have type 1 diabetes, your immune system mistakenly treats the beta cells in your pancreas that create insulin as foreign invaders and destroys them. When enough beta cells are destroyed, your pancreas can't make insulin or makes so little of it that you need to take insulin to live.

Insulin is an important hormone that regulates the amount of glucose (sugar) in your blood. Under normal circumstances, insulin functions in the following steps:

• Your body breaks down the food you eat into glucose (sugar), which is your body's main source of energy.

• Glucose enters your bloodstream, which signals your pancreas to release insulin.

• Insulin helps glucose in your blood enter your muscle, fat and liver cells so they can use it for energy or store it for later use.

• When glucose enters your cells and the levels in your bloodstream decrease, it signals your pancreas to stop producing insulin.

If you have diabetes, blood glucose can't enter your cells so it builds up in your bloodstream. This causes high blood glucose (hyperglycemia). Over time, high blood glucose harms your body and can lead to diabetes-related complications if not treated.

Most of the time, type 1 diabetes is diagnosed in young people, but it can develop in anyone at any age. Scientists and researchers today aren't sure how to prevent type 1 diabetes or what triggers it.

If you have type 1 diabetes, you can live a long, healthy life by having a strong support system and managing it with your diabetes care team. The treatment plan you develop with your diabetes care team will include insulin, physical activity, and an eating plan to reach your health goals.

Type 1 diabetes vs. secondary diabetes

A condition called secondary diabetes is like type 1, but your insulin-making cells are wiped out by another health condition or an injury to your pancreas, rather than by your immune system.

Type 1 diabetes vs. type 2 diabetes

If you have type 1, your body doesn't make enough insulin. With type 2 diabetes, your body can make insulin but can't use it well. The cells in your muscles, fat, and liver build up what's called insulin resistance.

With type 1 diabetes, you need to use man-made insulin every day so your body can function. But not everyone with type 2 diabetes needs it. Other medications can help you manage the condition.

4

No matter which type of diabetes you have, you'll need to keep a close eye on your daily habits, such as what you eat and how much activity you get to stay healthy.

Who does Type 1 diabetes affect?

Anyone at any age can develop Type 1 diabetes (T1D), though the most common age at diagnosis is between the ages of 4 to 6 and in early puberty (10 to 14 years).

In the United States, people who are non-Hispanic white are most likely to get Type 1 diabetes, and it affects people assigned female at birth and people assigned male at birth almost equally.

While you don't have to have a family member with Type 1 diabetes to develop the condition, having a first-degree family member (parent or sibling) with Type 1 diabetes increases your risk of developing it.

How common is Type 1 diabetes?

Type 1 diabetes is relatively common. In the United States, approximately 1.24 million people live with Type 1 diabetes, and that number is expected to grow to five million by 2050.

Type 1 diabetes is one of the most common chronic diseases that affect children in the United States, though adults can be diagnosed with the disease as well.

Type 1 Diabetes Symptoms

Symptoms can come on very quickly. They include:

- Extreme thirst
- Increased hunger (especially after eating)
- Dry mouth
- Upset stomach and vomiting
- Frequent peeing
- Unexplained weight loss (despite eating and often feeling hungry)
- Feeling tired or weak for no reason
- Vision changes
- Heavy, labored breathing (your doctor may call this Kussmaul respiration)
- Repeated infections of your skin, urinary tract, or vagina
- Mood changes

Late-onset type 1 diabetes symptoms

More research is being done on what's called Latent Autoimmune Diabetes in Adults (LADA).

Some people refer to this as "Diabetes 1.5" or "Diabetes 1 1/2" because it overlaps with parts of both type 1 and type 2 diabetes.

LADA symptoms can come on very slowly, making it tricky to diagnose. So does the fact that people who have it are usually at a healthy weight, and often between the ages of 30 and 50 years.

Balanced Nutrition for Type 1 Diabetes

Following a healthy diet has many benefits, including building strong bones, protecting the heart, preventing disease, and boosting mood.

A healthy diet typically includes nutrient-dense foods from all of the major food groups, including lean proteins, whole grains, healthy fats, and fruits and vegetables of many colors. Healthy eating habits also include replacing foods that contain trans fats, added salt, and sugar with more nutritious options.

Following a healthy diet has many benefits, including building strong bones, protecting the heart, preventing disease, and boosting the mood.

Diabetes management

A healthy diet may help a person with diabetes:

• manage their blood glucose levels

• keep their blood pressure and cholesterol within target ranges

• prevent or delay complications of diabetes

• maintain a moderate weight

It is vital for people with diabetes to limit their intake of foods with added sugar and salt. They should also consider avoiding fried foods high in saturated and trans fats.

Heart health

According to the Centers for Disease Control and Prevention (CDC), heart disease is the leading cause of death for adults in the United States.

The American Heart Association (AHA) states that almost half of U.S. adults live with some form of cardiovascular disease.

High blood pressure, or hypertension, is a growing concern in the U.S. The condition can lead to a heart attack, heart failure, and a stroke.

It may be possible to prevent up to 80% of premature heart disease and stroke diagnoses with lifestyle changes, such as increasing physical activity and healthful eating.

The foods people eat can reduce their blood pressure and help keep their hearts healthy.

The DASH diet, or the Dietary Approaches to Stop Hypertension diet, includes plenty of heart healthy foods. The program recommends:

• eating plenty of vegetables, fruits, and whole grains

• choosing fat-free or low fat dairy products, fish, poultry, beans, nuts, and vegetable oils

• limiting saturated and trans fat intake, such as fatty meats and full-fat dairy products

• limiting drinks and foods that contain added sugars

• restricting sodium intake to less than 2,300 milligrams per day — ideally 1,500 mg daily — and increasing consumption of potassium, magnesium, and calcium

High-fiber foods are also crucial for keeping the heart healthy.

The AHA states that dietary fiber helps improve blood cholesterol and lowers the risk of heart disease, stroke, obesity, and type 2 diabetes.

The medical community has long recognized the link between trans fats and heart-related illnesses, such as coronary heart disease.

Limiting certain types of fats can also improve heart health. For instance, eliminating trans fats reduces the levels of low-density lipoprotein (LDL) cholesterol. This type of cholesterol causes plaque to collect within the arteries, increasing the risk of a heart attack and stroke.

Reducing blood pressure can also promote heart health. Most adults may achieve this by limiting their salt intake to no more than 1,500 mg per day.

Food manufacturers add salt to many processed and fast foods, and a person who wishes to lower their blood pressure should avoid these products.

Reduced cancer risk

A person may eat foods that contain antioxidants to help reduce their risk of developing cancer by protecting their cells from damage.

The presence of free radicals in the body increases the risk of cancer, but antioxidants help remove them to lower the likelihood of this disease.

Many phytochemicals found in fruits, vegetables, nuts, and legumes act as antioxidants, including beta carotene, lycopene, and vitamins A, C, and E.

According to the National Cancer Institute, there are laboratory and animal studies that link certain antioxidants to a reduced incidence of free radical damage due to cancer. However, human trials are inconclusive and doctors advise against using these dietary supplements without consulting them first.

Foods high in antioxidants include:

- Berries, such as blueberries and raspberries
- Dark, leafy greens
- Pumpkin and carrots
- Nuts and seeds

Having obesity may increase a person's risk of developing cancer and result in poorer outcomes. Maintaining a moderate weight may reduce these risks.

In a 2014 study, researchers found that a diet rich in fruits reduced the risk of upper gastrointestinal tract cancers.

They also found that a diet rich in vegetables, fruits, and fiber lowered the risk of colorectal cancer, while a diet rich in fiber reduces the risk of liver cancer.

Better mood

Some evidence suggests a close relationship between diet and mood.

In 2016, researchers found that diets with a high glycemic load may trigger increased symptoms of depression and fatigue in people who have obesity but are otherwise healthy.

A diet with a high glycemic load includes many refined carbohydrates, such as those found in soft drinks, cakes, white bread, and biscuits. Vegetables, whole fruit, and whole grains have a lower glycemic load.

Recent research also found that diet can affect blood glucose levels, immune activation, and the gut microbiome, which may affect a person's mood. The researchers also found that there may be a link between more healthful diets, such as the Mediterranean diet, and better mental health. Whereas, the opposite is true for diets with high amounts of red meat, processed, and high fat foods.

It is important to note that the researchers highlighted a necessity for further research into the mechanisms that link food and mental health.

If a person suspects they have symptoms of depression, talking with a doctor or mental health professional may help.

Improved gut health

The colon is full of naturally occurring bacteria, which play important roles in metabolism and digestion.

Certain strains of bacteria also produce vitamins K and B, which benefit the colon. They may also help fight harmful bacteria and viruses.

A diet high in fiber may decrease inflammation in the gut. A diet rich in fibrous vegetables, fruits, legumes, and whole grains may provide a combination of prebiotics and probiotics that help good bacteria thrive in the colon.

These fermented foods are rich in probiotics:

- Yogurt
- Kimchi
- Sauerkraut

- Miso
- Kefir

Prebiotics may help improve a range of digestive issues, including irritable bowel syndrome (IBS) symptoms.

Improved memory

A healthful diet may help maintain cognition and brain health. However, further conclusive research is necessary.

A 2015 study identified nutrients and foods that protect against cognitive decline and dementia. The researchers found the following to be beneficial:

- Vitamin D, C, and E
- Omega-3 fatty acids

- Flavonoids and polyphenols
- Fish

Among other diets, the Mediterranean diet incorporates many of these nutrients.

Weight loss

Maintaining a moderate weight can help reduce the risk of chronic health issues. A person who has more weight or obesity may be at risk of developing certain conditions, including:

- Coronary heart disease
- Type 2 diabetes
- Osteoarthritis
- Stroke
- Hypertension
- Certain mental health conditions

- Some cancers

Many healthful foods, including vegetables, fruits, and beans, are lower in calories than most processed foods.

A person can determine their calorie requirements using guidance from the Dietary Guidelines for Americans 2020–2025.

Maintaining a healthy diet can help a person stay within their daily limit without monitoring their calorie intake.

In 2018, researchers found that following a diet rich in fiber and lean proteins resulted in weight loss without the need for monitoring calorie intake.

Strong bones and teeth

A diet with adequate calcium and magnesium is important for strong bones and teeth. Keeping the bones healthy can minimize the risk of bone issues later in life, such as osteoporosis.

The following foods are rich in calcium:

- Dairy products
- Kale
- Broccoli
- Canned fish with bones

Food manufacturers often fortify cereals, tofu, and plant-based milk with calcium.

Magnesium is abundant in many foods, and some of the best sources include:

- Leafy green vegetables
- Nuts

- Seeds
- Whole grains

Getting better sleep

A variety of factors, including sleep apnea, can disrupt sleep patterns.

Sleep apnea occurs when a condition repeatedly blocks the airways during sleep. Risk factors include obesity and drinking alcohol.

Reducing alcohol and caffeine intake may help a person gain restful sleep, whether they have sleep apnea or not.

The health of the next generation

Children learn most health-related behaviors from the adults around them, and parents who model healthy eating and exercise habits tend to pass these on.

Eating at home may also help. In 2018, researchers found that children who regularly ate meals with their families consumed more vegetables and fewer sugary foods than their peers, who ate at home less frequently.

Quick tips for a healthful diet

There are plenty of small ways to improve a person's diet, including:

• swapping soft drinks for water or herbal tea

• ensuring each meal consists of some fresh produce

• choosing whole grains instead of refined carbohydrates

• consuming whole fruits instead of juices

• limiting red and processed meats, which are high in salt and may increase the risk of colon cancer

• eating more lean protein, which people can find in eggs, tofu, fish, and nuts

A person may also benefit from taking a cooking class and learning how to incorporate more vegetables into their meals.

Tips for Managing Blood Sugar with Diet

A diet rich in vegetables, fruits, and lean proteins can benefit a person with diabetes. At the same time, a person with diabetes may need to limit their intake of white bread, sweets, and other highly refined foods.

Both sugary and starchy carbohydrates can raise blood sugar. But these foods, in the right amounts, can play a role in a balanced meal plan. The right amount and type of carbohydrates can depend on many factors, including a person's activity level and medications, such as insulin.

Green, leafy vegetables

Green, leafy vegetables are a key plant-based source of potassium, vitamin A, and calcium. They also provide protein and fiber.

Some researchers have found that eating green, leafy vegetables can benefit people with diabetes due to these plants' high antioxidant and fiber content.

Green, leafy vegetables include:

- Spinach
- Collard greens
- Kale
- Cabbage
- Bok choy
- Broccoli

Whole grains

Whole grains contain high levels of fiber and more nutrients than refined white grains.

Eating a diet high in fiber is important for people with diabetes because fiber slows the digestion process. Slower absorption of nutrients helps keep blood sugar stable.

Whole wheat and whole grains are lower on the glycemic index (GI) scale than white breads and rice. This means that they have less of an effect on blood sugar.

Good examples of whole grains to include in the diet are:

- Brown rice
- Whole grain bread
- Whole grain pasta

- Buckwheat
- Quinoa
- Millet
- Bulgur
- Rye

Fatty fish

Fatty fish is a beneficial addition to any diet. It contains important omega-3 fatty acids called eicosapentaenoic acid and docosahexaenoic acid. These are sometimes known as EPA and DHA.

People need certain amounts of healthy fats to keep their body functioning and to promote heart and brain health.

The American Diabetes Association (ADA) reports that a Mediterranean diet, a dietary plan high in polyunsaturated and monounsaturated fats may improve blood sugar management and blood lipids in people with diabetes.

Certain fish are a rich source of both polyunsaturated and monounsaturated fats. These are:

- Salmon
- Mackerel
- Sardines
- Albacore tuna
- Herring
- Trout

People can eat seaweeds, such as kelp and spirulina, as plant-based alternative sources of these fatty acids.

Beans

Beans are an excellent option for people with diabetes. They are a source of plant-based protein and can help satisfy the appetite while helping promote digestive health due to their high content of soluble fibers.

Beans are also low on the GI scale, which means they may be more effective for blood sugar management than many other starchy foods.

Among the many types of beans are:

- Kidney
- Pinto
- Black
- Navy
- Adzuki

Beans also contain important nutrients, including iron, potassium, and magnesium.

Walnuts

Nuts can be another excellent addition to the diet. As with fish, nuts contain fatty acids that help keep the heart healthy.

Walnuts are especially rich in a type of omega-3 called alpha-linolenic acid (ALA). As with other omega-3s, ALA is important for heart health. People with diabetes may have a higher risk of heart disease or stroke, so it is important to consume these fatty acids.

A study from 2021 suggested that eating walnuts has links with a lower incidence of diabetes.

Walnuts also provide key nutrients, such as protein, vitamin B6, magnesium, and iron.

Citrus fruits

Eating these fruits can be an easy way to get vitamins and minerals. The ADA notes that citrus fruits, such as oranges, grapefruits, and lemons, can benefit people with diabetes.

Some researchers have found that citrus fruits are rich in many flavonoid antioxidants, such as hesperidin and naringin, which may exhibit antidiabetic effects.

Citrus fruits are also a great source of:

- Vitamin C
- Folate
- Potassium

Berries

Berries are full of antioxidants, which can help prevent oxidative stress. Oxidative stress has links with a wide range of health conditions, including heart disease and some cancers.

Studies have found that oxidative stress contributes to type 2 diabetes. This occurs when there is an imbalance between antioxidants and unstable molecules called free radicals in the body.

Blueberries, blackberries, strawberries, and raspberries all contain antioxidants and fiber. They also contain important other vitamins and minerals, including:

- Vitamin C
- Vitamin K

- Manganese
- Potassium

Sweet potatoes

Sweet potatoes rank lower on the GI scale than white potatoes. This makes them a great alternative for people with diabetes, as they release sugar more slowly and do not raise blood sugar as much. They are also a good source of fiber, which also helps with blood sugar regulation.

Sweet potatoes are also a great source of:

- Vitamin A
- Vitamin C
- Potassium

Probiotic yogurt

Probiotics are the helpful bacteria that live in the human gut and improve digestion and overall health.

A small 2022 study found that people with type 2 diabetes and obesity who took probiotics supplements for 90 days had better blood sugar levels, higher levels of "good" cholesterol (also called HDL cholesterol), and healthier gut bacteria.

Another 2020 meta-analysis of 15 clinical trials found that probiotics may reduce insulin resistance, fasting blood sugar, and HbA1c (a measure of blood sugar management over a 3–4-month period) in people with diabetes.

A person should consider choosing a plain variety with no added sugar. Probiotic yogurt contains live, active cultures such as Lactobacillus and Bifidobacterium, which it may advertise on the label.

Chia seeds

People often call chia seeds a superfood because of their high antioxidant and omega-3 content. They are also a good source of plant-based protein and fiber.

In one small-scale trial from 2017, people who had overweight and type 2 diabetes lost more weight after 6 months when they included chia seeds in their diets compared with those who ate an oat bran alternative. The researchers support the beneficial role of chia seeds helping people with type 2 diabetes to manage their weight more effectively.

Obesity is a significant risk factor for diabetes, and weight loss can help with improved blood sugar management.

What is a good diet for people with diabetes?

According to the ADA, a beneficial foods for people with diabetes includes the following:

- Fruits and vegetables
- Lean protein
- Foods with less added sugar
- Fewer processed foods

Although, as the ADA also reports, no single diet offers more benefits to a person with diabetes than another.

However, research suggests that a low carbohydrate diet may be useful. It may help reduce cravings, lower blood sugar, and boost energy. It may also help people with diabetes maintain a moderate weight.

Low carb diets also have variations, including:

- Keto diet
- Mediterranean diet
- Paleo diet
- Vegetarian or vegan diet

Foods to limit

One way to manage diabetes with dietary changes is to balance high and low GI foods. High GI foods increase blood sugar more than low GI foods.

When choosing high GI foods, limit portions and pair them with sources of protein or healthy fats to reduce their effect on blood sugar and feel fuller for longer.

Foods high on the GI scale include:

- White bread
- Puffed rice
- White rice
- White pasta
- White potatoes
- Chocolate
- Cookies
- Cakes
- Potato chips
- Regular soda

People with diabetes may also wish to limit or balance portions of the following foods:

Carb-heavy foods

Carbohydrates (carbs) are an important part of all meals. However, people with diabetes may benefit from limiting their carb intake or pairing carbs with a healthy protein or fat source.

Saturated and trans fats

Certain fats, such as saturated and trans fats, may increase insulin resistance and contribute to reduced blood sugar management in people with diabetes. Many fried and processed foods, including fries, chips, and baked goods, contain these types of fats.

Refined sugar

People with diabetes should limit or avoid sources of refined sugar, such as store-bought or homemade sweets, cakes, and biscuits.

The American Heart Association recommends consuming no more than 25 g or 6 teaspoons (tsp) of added sugar per day for females, and 36 g or 9 tsp for males. This does not include naturally occurring sugars from foods such as fruit or plain milk.

Sugary drinks

Drinks that contain a lot of sugar, such as energy drinks, some coffees, and shakes, can disrupt a person's insulin level, leading to an imbalance.

Salty foods

Foods that are high in salt can raise blood pressure. Salt may appear as "sodium" on a food label.

The ADA recommends limiting the sodium intake to under 2,300 milligrams (mg) per day, regardless of a person's diabetes status.

Alcohol

Drinking alcohol in moderation should not carry serious risks for people with diabetes and should not affect long-term glucose management.

However, people with diabetes should avoid mixed drinks or cocktails as these often contain added sugars that can lead to blood sugar spikes.

People prescribed insulin or insulin secretagogue therapies may have a higher risk of hypoglycemia linked to alcohol consumption.

The Centers for Disease Control and Prevention (CDC) recommends that females who drink alcohol limit it to one drink per day and that males limit it to two drinks per day, regardless of diabetes status.

Chapter 2: Type 1 Diabetes in Children

Type 1 diabetes in children is a condition in which your child's body no longer produces an important hormone (insulin). Your child needs insulin to survive, so the missing insulin needs to be replaced with injections or with an insulin pump. Type 1 diabetes in children used to be known as juvenile diabetes or insulin-dependent diabetes.

The diagnosis of type 1 diabetes in children can be overwhelming, especially in the beginning. Suddenly you and your child — depending on your child's age — must learn how to give injections, count carbohydrates and monitor blood sugar.

There's no cure for type 1 diabetes in children, but it can be managed. Advances in blood sugar monitoring and insulin delivery have improved blood sugar management and quality of life for children with type 1 diabetes.

Your child is at higher risk of type 1 diabetes if:

They're aged 4-6 years or 10-14 years.

Another family member also has it.

Type 1 diabetes symptoms in children

The signs are the same as for adults, but you may also notice:

• More diaper changes for a baby

- Diaper rash that doesn't get better when treated
- Bed-wetting in kids who are potty-trained
- Fast breathing
- Belly pain
- Throwing up
- Behavior changes
- Fruity-smelling breath

In some babies or kids, type 1 diabetes can also look like the flu.

If you notice any of these symptoms, take your child to the doctor.

Causes

The exact cause of type 1 diabetes is unknown. But in most people with type 1 diabetes, the body's immune system — which normally fights harmful bacteria and viruses — mistakenly destroys insulin-producing (islet) cells in the pancreas. Genetics and environmental factors appear to play a role in this process.

Once the islet cells of the pancreas are destroyed, your child produces little or no insulin. Insulin performs the critical job of moving sugar (glucose) from the bloodstream to the body's cells for energy.

Sugar enters the bloodstream when food is digested. Without enough insulin, sugar builds up in your child's bloodstream. This can cause life-threatening complications if left untreated.

Risk factors

Type 1 diabetes most often occurs in children but can occur at any age. Risk factors for type 1 diabetes in children include:

• **Family history.** Anyone with a parent or siblings with type 1 diabetes has a slightly increased risk of developing the condition.

• **Genetics.** Certain genes indicate an increased risk of type 1 diabetes.

• **Race.** In the United States, type 1 diabetes is more common among white children of non-Hispanic descent than among children of other races.

• **Certain viruses.** Exposure to various viruses may trigger the autoimmune destruction of the islet cells.

Complications

Type 1 diabetes can affect the major organs in your body. Keeping your blood sugar level close to normal most of the time can dramatically reduce the risk of many complications.

Complications can include:

• **Heart and blood vessel disease.** Diabetes increases your child's risk of developing conditions such as narrowed blood vessels, high blood pressure, heart disease and stroke later in life.

• **Nerve damage.** Excess sugar can injure the walls of the tiny blood vessels that nourish your child's nerves. This can cause tingling, numbness, burning or pain. Nerve damage usually happens gradually over a long period of time.

• **Kidney damage.** Diabetes can damage the numerous tiny blood vessel clusters in the kidneys that filter waste from your child's blood.

• **Eye damage.** Diabetes can damage the blood vessels of the eye's retina, which may lead to vision problems.

• **Osteoporosis**. Diabetes may decrease bone mineral density, increasing your child's risk of osteoporosis as an adult.

You can help your child prevent diabetes complications by:

• Working with your child to maintain good blood sugar control as much as possible

• Teaching your child the importance of eating a healthy diet and participating in regular physical activity

• Scheduling regular visits with your child's diabetes health care professional

Children with type 1 diabetes are at risk of other autoimmune disorders, such as thyroid disease and celiac disease. Your child's health care provider may recommend tests for these conditions.

Prevention

There's currently no sure way to prevent type 1 diabetes, but this is a very active area of research.

The antibodies associated with type 1 diabetes in children who have a high risk of the disorder can be detected months or even years before the first symptoms of type 1 diabetes appear. Researchers are working on:

• Preventing or delaying the start of type 1 diabetes in people who have a high risk of the disease.

• Preventing further destruction of the islet cells in people who are newly diagnosed.

Diagnosis

There are several blood tests for type 1 diabetes in children. These tests are used to diagnose diabetes and to monitor diabetes management:

• **Random blood sugar test.** This is the primary screening test for type 1 diabetes. A blood sample is taken at a random time. A blood sugar level of

200 milligrams per deciliter (mg/dL), or 11.1 millimoles per liter (mmol/L), or higher, along with symptoms, suggests diabetes.

- **Glycated hemoglobin (A1C) test.** This test indicates your child's average blood sugar level for the past 3 months. An A1C level of 6.5% or higher on two separate tests indicates diabetes.

- **Fasting blood sugar test.** A blood sample is taken after your child hasn't eaten (fasted) for at least 8 hours or overnight. A fasting blood sugar level of 126 mg/dL (7.0 mmol/L) or higher suggests type 1 diabetes.

Additional tests

If blood sugar testing indicates diabetes, your health care provider may recommend additional tests to distinguish between type 1 diabetes and type 2 diabetes because treatment strategies differ by type. Additional tests include blood tests to check for antibodies that are common in type 1 diabetes.

Treatment

Treatment for type 1 diabetes includes:

• Taking insulin

• Monitoring blood sugar

• Eating healthy foods

• Exercising regularly

You'll work closely with your child's diabetes treatment team — health care provider, certified diabetes care and education specialist, and registered dietitian. The goal of treatment is to keep your child's blood sugar within certain numbers. This target range helps to keep your child's blood sugar level as close to normal as possible.

Your child's health care provider will let you know what your child's blood sugar target range is. This range may change as your child grows and changes.

Insulin

Anyone who has type 1 diabetes needs lifelong treatment with one or more types of insulin to survive.

Many types of insulin are available, including:

- **Rapid-acting insulin**. This type of insulin starts working within 15 minutes. It reaches peak effect at 60 minutes and lasts about 4 hours. This type is often used 15 to 20 minutes before meals. Examples are lispro (Humalog, Admelog), aspart (NovoLog, Fiasp) and glulisine (Apidra).

- **Short-acting insulin.** Sometimes called regular insulin, this type starts working around 30 minutes after injection. It reaches peak effect at 90 to 120 minutes and lasts about 4 to 6 hours. Examples are human insulin (Humulin R, Novolin R).

- **Intermediate-acting insulin.** Also called NPH insulin, this type of insulin starts working in about 1 to 3 hours. It reaches peak effect at 6 to 8 hours and lasts 12 to 24 hours. Examples are NPH insulin (Humulin N, Novolin N).

• **Long- and ultra-long-acting insulin.** This type of insulin may provide coverage for as long as 14 to 40 hours. Examples are glargine (Lantus, Toujeo, other), detemir (Levemir) and degludec (Tresiba).

Insulin delivery options

Insulin delivery options include:

• **Fine needle and syringe.** This looks like a shot you might get in a health care provider's office, but with a smaller syringe and a much thinner, shorter needle.

• **Insulin pen with fine needle.** This device looks like an ink pen, except the cartridge is filled with insulin. A needle is attached for injection.

• **An insulin pump**. This is a small device worn on the outside of your body that you program to deliver specific amounts of insulin throughout the day and when you eat. A tube connects a reservoir of insulin to a catheter that's inserted under the skin of your abdomen.

There's also a tubeless pump option that involves wearing a pod containing the insulin on your body combined with a tiny catheter that's inserted under your skin.

Blood sugar monitoring

You or your child will need to check and record your child's blood sugar at least four times a day. Typically, you or your child test his or her blood glucose before every meal and at bedtime and occasionally during the middle of the night. But you or your child may need to check it more often if your child doesn't have a continuous glucose monitor.

Frequent testing is the only way to make sure that your child's blood sugar level remains within the target range.

Continuous glucose monitoring (CGM)

Continuous glucose monitoring (CGM) devices measure your blood sugar every few minutes using a temporary sensor inserted under the skin. Some devices show your blood sugar reading at all times on a receiver or your smartphone or smartwatch, while others require that you check your blood sugar by running the receiver over the sensor.

Closed loop system

A closed loop system is a device implanted in the body that links a continuous glucose monitor to an insulin pump. The monitor checks blood sugar levels regularly. The device automatically delivers the right amount of insulin when the monitor shows that it's needed.

The Food and Drug Administration has approved several hybrid closed loop systems for type 1 diabetes. They are called "hybrid" because these systems require some input from the user. For example, you may have to tell the device how many carbohydrates are eaten, or confirm blood sugar levels from time to time.

A closed loop system that doesn't need any user input isn't available yet. But more of these systems currently are in clinical trials.

What Should Kids with Diabetes Eat?

Food is a big part of any diabetes treatment plan, but that doesn't mean your child has to follow a strict "diabetes diet." Just like the rest of the family, your child's diet should regularly include foods that are high in nutrition and low in fat and calories, such as:

• Vegetables

• Fruits

• Lean protein

• Whole grains

Your child's registered dietitian can help you create a meal plan that fits your child's food preferences and health goals, as well as help you plan for occasional treats. The dietitian will also teach you how to count carbohydrates in foods so that you can use that information when figuring out insulin doses.

Healthy Lifestyle Practices for Children with Diabetes

Physical activity

Everyone needs regular aerobic exercise, and children who have type 1 diabetes are no exception.

But remember that physical activity can affect blood sugar. This effect on blood sugar levels can remain for hours after exercise, possibly even overnight. You or your child might need to adjust your child's meal plan or insulin doses for the increased activity.

If your child begins a new activity, check your child's blood sugar more often than usual until you and your child learn how his or her body reacts to the activity.

Make physical activity part of your child's daily routine. Encourage your child to get at least 60 minutes of physical activity daily or, better yet, exercise with your child.

Handling Type 1 Diabetes Challenges in Kids

Blood sugar can sometimes change unpredictably. During these challenges, more frequent blood sugar testing can help identify problems and guide treatment. Ask your child's diabetes treatment team how to handle these and other challenges:

• **Picky eating.** Very young children with type 1 diabetes might not finish what's on their plates, which can be a problem if they've already received insulin for that food.

• **Illness.** Sickness has varying effects on children's insulin needs. Hormones produced during illness raise blood sugar levels, but reduced carbohydrate intake due to poor appetite or vomiting lowers the insulin requirement. Your child's health care provider will recommend a flu shot for your child every year and may recommend the pneumonia vaccine as well as the COVID-19 vaccine if your child is age 5 or older.

• **Growth spurts and puberty.** Just when you've mastered your child's insulin needs, he or she sprouts up seemingly overnight, and suddenly isn't getting enough insulin. Hormones also can affect insulin requirements, particularly for teenage females as they begin to menstruate.

• **Sleep**. To avoid problems with low blood sugar during the night, you might need to adjust your child's insulin routine and snack times.

• **Temporary changes in routine.** Despite planning, days don't always stay the same. Check blood sugars often when schedules change unexpectedly. Plan ahead for holidays, special occasions and vacations.

Ongoing medical care

Your child will need regular appointments to ensure good diabetes management. This can include a review of your child's blood sugar patterns, insulin needs, eating and physical activity.

Your health care provider also checks your child's A1C levels. The American Diabetes Association generally recommends an A1C of 7% or lower for all children and teens with diabetes.

Your health care provider also will periodically check your child's:

- Blood pressure

- Growth

- Cholesterol levels

- Thyroid function

- Kidney function

- Feet

- Eyes

Signs of Type 1 Diabetes Complications in Kids

Despite your best efforts, sometimes problems will arise. Certain short-term complications of type 1 diabetes require immediate care or they could become very serious, including:

• Low blood sugar (hypoglycemia)

• High blood sugar (hyperglycemia)

• Diabetic ketoacidosis (DKA)

Low blood sugar (hypoglycemia)

Hypoglycemia is a blood sugar level below your child's target range. Blood sugar levels can drop for many reasons, including skipping a meal, getting more physical activity than typical or injecting too much insulin. Low blood sugar is not uncommon in people with type 1 diabetes, but if it isn't treated quickly, symptoms will get worse.

Signs and symptoms of low blood sugar include:

• Pallor

• Shakiness

• Hunger

• Sweating

• Irritability and other mood changes

• Difficulty concentrating or confusion

• Dizziness or lightheadedness

• Loss of coordination

• Slurred speech

• Loss of consciousness

• Seizures

Teach your child the symptoms of low blood sugar. When in doubt, he or she should always do a blood sugar test. If a blood glucose meter isn't readily available and your child is having symptoms of a low blood sugar, treat for low blood sugar, and then test as soon as possible.

If your child has a low blood sugar reading:

• **Give a fast-acting carbohydrate**. Have your child consume 15 to 20 grams of a fast-acting carbohydrate, such as fruit juice, glucose tablets, hard candy, regular (not diet) soda or another source of sugar. Foods with added fat, such as chocolate or ice cream, don't raise blood sugar as quickly because fat slows down the absorption of the sugar.

• **Retest blood sugar.** Retest your child's blood sugar in about 15 minutes to make sure it's back in the target range. If it's not, repeat giving a fast-acting carbohydrate and testing in 15 minutes as needed until you get a reading in your child's target range.

• **Follow up with a snack or meal.** Once the blood sugar is back in the target range, have your child eat a healthy snack or a meal to help prevent another low blood sugar level.

If a low blood sugar causes your child to lose consciousness, an emergency injection of a hormone that stimulates the release of sugar into the blood (glucagon) may be necessary.

High blood sugar (hyperglycemia)

Hyperglycemia is a blood sugar level above your child's target range. Blood sugar levels can rise for many reasons, including illness, eating too much, eating certain types of foods and not taking enough insulin.

Signs and symptoms of high blood sugar include:

• Frequent urination

• Increased thirst or dry mouth

• Blurred vision

• Fatigue

• Nausea

If you suspect a high blood sugar level, test your child's blood sugar. If the blood sugar is higher than the target range, follow your child's diabetes treatment plan or check with your child's health care provider. High blood sugar levels don't come down quickly, so ask how long to wait until you check the blood sugar again.

If your child has a blood sugar reading above 240 mg/dL (13.3 mmol/L), your child should use an over-the-counter ketone test kit to check for ketones.

Diabetic ketoacidosis (DKA)

A severe lack of insulin causes your child's body to break down fat for energy. This causes the body to produce a substance called ketones. Excess ketones build up in your child's blood, creating a potentially life-threatening condition known as diabetic ketoacidosis.

Signs and symptoms of DKA include:

• Thirst or very dry mouth

• Increased urination

• Dry or flushed skin

• Nausea, vomiting or abdominal pain

• A sweet, fruity smell on your child's breath

• Confusion

If you suspect DKA, check your child's urine for excess ketones. If the ketone levels are high, call your child's health care provider or seek emergency care.

What is the honeymoon phase in type 1 diabetes?

The honeymoon period can occur right after an initial diagnosis of type 1 diabetes, and when a person starts insulin treatment.

At this time, diabetes may seem to go into remission or disappear.

Type 1 diabetes is the result of a faulty immune reaction against the pancreas, the organ that produces insulin. The immune system usually destroys unwanted substances, such as bacteria, but sometimes it can go wrong and destroy healthy cells instead.

When a person first receives a diagnosis of type 1 diabetes, some of their insulin-producing cells still function. While these cells continue to do their job, the body is still able to produce some insulin.

The need for synthetic or additional insulin may decrease when the person first starts treatment, and some people may be able to stop using it altogether.

This "honeymoon phase" may last from a few weeks to several months but will eventually end. It may seem that the diabetes has gone away, but, unfortunately, this is only a remission.

After a while, the remaining insulin-producing cells will stop working. As the person monitor their blood sugar, they will notice levels rising again. The need for synthetic insulin will increase.

In time, diabetes will destroy all the insulin-producing cells. As a result, the pancreas will no longer produce insulin, and the honeymoon period ends.

The person will not have another honeymoon period and will depend on external insulin.

Is there a honeymoon phase in type 2 diabetes?

Some people with type 2 diabetes may experience a reduction in symptoms and blood sugar levels after diagnosis, but this is not the same as a type 1 honeymoon phase.

Doctors may advise someone with a new diagnosis of prediabetes or type 2 diabetes to modify their diet and lifestyle. This may include getting regular exercise and eating a healthful diet.

These changes can lower a person's blood glucose levels.

However, if the person stops these healthful habits, blood glucose levels can rise again.

Honeymoon period duration

Diabetes affects individuals differently, and the honeymoon phase, too, varies between people. There is no standard time for it to last, and not everyone with type 1 diabetes will experience it.

The honeymoon phase usually occurs in the first 3 months after diagnosis.

Over a period of weeks to as much as a year or more, the immune system will continue to attack the pancreas and kill off the remaining cells that are producing insulin.

As more insulin-producing cells die, the honeymoon period comes to an end.

Blood sugar levels during the honeymoon period

During the honeymoon period, a person with diabetes may experience normal or near-normal blood sugar readings while taking no or minimal insulin.

Normal blood sugar levels, or plasma blood glucose readings, for people with diabetes, are:

• **After fasting**: 80–130 milligrams per deciliter (mg/dl)

• **1–2 hours after meals:** Less than 180 mg/dl

Each person should speak to a doctor to find out their own target levels for blood sugar, as different people will have different needs.

During the honeymoon period, a person with diabetes may regularly see blood sugar readings within the healthy range while taking little or no prescribed insulin.

However, over time, they will notice fewer readings within the normal level, signaling that the remaining insulin-producing cells no longer function and the honeymoon period may be ending.

Blood glucose testing kits are available for purchase online.

Potential future treatments

Pancreas transplant. With a successful pancreas transplant, you would no longer need insulin. But pancreas transplants aren't always successful — and the procedure poses serious risks. Because these risks can be more dangerous than the diabetes itself, pancreas transplants are generally used for those with very difficult-to-manage diabetes. They can also be used for people who also need a kidney transplant.

Islet cell transplantation. Researchers are experimenting with islet cell transplantation. This provides new insulin-producing cells from a donor pancreas. This experimental procedure had some problems in the past. But new techniques and better drugs to prevent islet cell rejection may improve its chances of becoming a successful treatment.

Chapter 3: Recommended Kid-Friendly Breakfast Recipes

Breakfast Sundae

Ingredients

1 small banana

4 ounces sugar-free, lowfat yogurt

1/3 cup granola cereal

1/4 cup seedless grapes, halved

Instructions

Peel banana and split lengthwise. Place in sundae dish or bowl. Top with yogurt. Sprinkle with cereal and fruit. Makes 1 serving.

1 serving = 1/2 milk + 2 fruit + 11/2 starch + 1 fat exchange or 58 grams of carbohydrate

Blender Breakfast

Ingredients

1/2 cup skim milk

1/2 cup low fat cottage cheese

1 cup frozen banana and strawberries, cubed

1 Tbsp. peanut butter

Instructions

Freeze bananas and strawberries until firm. Mix ingredients in blender and blend until smooth. Pour into glass. Makes 1 serving.

1 serving = 2 starch + 1/2 milk + 2 meat + 1 fat exchange or 38 grams of carbohydrate

Breakfast Eggnog

Ingredients

1 cup 2% milk

1/4 cup egg beaters

1 tsp. vanilla extract

1/2 banana

1/2 tsp. cinnamon, ground

1/2 tsp. nutmeg, ground

1 tsp. granulated artificial sweetener

1/2 tsp. brown sugar

Instructions

In a saucepan, warm milk over low heat. Combine all other ingredients in a blender. Add warmed milk and whip in blender for one minute. Serve in 16 ounce glass or mug. Makes 1 serving.

1 serving = 1 fruit + 1 milk + 1 meat exchange or 35 grams of carbohydrate

Nutty Banana

Ingredients

1/2 cup peanut butter

2 Tbsp. low fat milk

2 bananas

1/2 cup chopped nuts

Instructions

Mix peanut butter with milk and blend until smooth. Peel bananas and cut in half crosswise. Insert a stick into the flat end of each banana half. Spread banana with peanut butter mixture and roll in chopped nuts. Place on waxed paper and freeze for 2 hours or until firm. Makes 4 servings of 1/2 banana each.

1 serving = 1 fruit + 2 meat + 1 fat exchange or 15 grams of carbohydrate

Raisin Bread Sticks

Ingredients

4 tsp. margarine

4 slices raisin bread, un-iced

1 tsp. cinnamon

Instructions

Preheat oven to 350 degrees. Melt margarine and brush on slices of bread. Sprinkle with cinnamon. Cut bread into 4 slices each and place on cookie sheet. Bake for 5 minutes or until crisp. Makes 4 serving of 4 sticks each.

1 serving = 1 starch + 1 fat exchange or 15 grams of carbohydrate

Mango Raspberry Smoothie

Ingredients

- ½ cup water

- ¼ medium avocado

- 1 tablespoon lemon juice

- ¾ cup frozen mango

- ¼ cup frozen raspberries

- 1 tablespoon agave (Optional)

Directions

1. Add water, avocado, lemon juice, mango, raspberries and agave (if using) to a blender. Blend until smooth.

Healthy Carrot Cake Muffins

Ingredients

- 1 ¾ cups whole-wheat pastry flour

- 1 ½ teaspoons baking powder

- 1 ½ teaspoons ground cinnamon

- ½ teaspoon baking soda

- ¼ teaspoon ground ginger

- ¼ teaspoon salt

- 2 large eggs

- ½ cup unsweetened applesauce

- ½ cup light brown sugar

- ¼ cup granulated sugar

- ½ cup plain whole-milk Greek yogurt, plus 2 tablespoons, divided

- 1 ½ cups grated carrots (about 3 medium carrots)

- ½ cup toasted chopped walnuts

- ⅓ cup unsifted confectioners' sugar

- 1 ½ ounces reduced-fat cream cheese, softened

Directions

1. Preheat oven to 375 degrees F. Line a 12-cup muffin tin with paper liners; coat with cooking spray. Set aside. Whisk flour, baking powder, cinnamon, baking soda, ginger and salt in a medium bowl. Whisk eggs, applesauce, brown sugar, granulated sugar and 1/2 cup yogurt in a large bowl; fold in carrots, walnuts and half of the flour mixture until combined. Add the remaining flour mixture; fold until just incorporated (some lumps can remain).

2. Fill the prepared muffin cups three-quarters full with batter (about 1/3 cup each). Bake until the muffins are golden and a wooden pick inserted in the centers comes out clean, about 18 minutes. Transfer to a wire rack; let cool completely, about 20 minutes.

3. Whisk confectioners' sugar, cream cheese and the remaining 2 tablespoons yogurt in a small bowl; whisk in 2 to 3 teaspoons water to reach desired frosting consistency. Dollop and spread the frosting over the cooled muffins.

Tips

To make ahead: Wrap airtight and refrigerate for up to 2 days. To freeze, wrap unfrosted muffins tightly in plastic wrap or foil; freeze for up to 3 months. Thaw completely before frosting.

Baked Banana-Nut Oatmeal Cups

Ingredients

- 3 cups rolled oats (see Tip)

- 1 ½ cups low-fat milk

- 2 ripe bananas, mashed (about 3/4 cup)

- ⅓ cup packed brown sugar

- 2 large eggs, lightly beaten

- 1 teaspoon baking powder

- 1 teaspoon ground cinnamon

- 1 teaspoon vanilla extract

- ½ teaspoon salt

- ½ cup toasted chopped pecans

Directions

1. Preheat oven to 375°F. Coat a muffin tin with cooking spray.

2. Combine oats, milk, bananas, brown sugar, eggs, baking powder, cinnamon, vanilla and salt in a large bowl. Fold in pecans. Divide the mixture among the muffin cups (about 1/3 cup each). Bake until a toothpick inserted in the center comes out clean, about 25 minutes. Cool in the pan for 10 minutes, then turn out onto a wire rack. Serve warm or at room temperature.

Really Green Smoothie

Ingredients

- 1 large ripe banana

- 1 cup packed baby kale or coarsely chopped mature kale

- 1 cup unsweetened vanilla almond milk

- ¼ ripe avocado

- 1 tablespoon chia seeds

- 2 teaspoons honey

- 1 cup ice cubes

Directions

1. Combine banana, kale, almond milk, avocado, chia seeds and honey in a blender. Blend on high until creamy and smooth. Add ice and blend until smooth.

Mango-Almond Smoothie Bowl

Ingredients

- ½ cup frozen chopped mango

- ½ cup nonfat plain Greek yogurt

- ¼ cup frozen sliced banana

- ¼ cup plain unsweetened almond milk

- 5 tablespoons unsalted almonds, divided

- ⅛ teaspoon ground allspice

- ¼ cup raspberries

- ½ teaspoon honey

Directions

1. Blend mango, yogurt, banana, almond milk, 3 tablespoons almonds and allspice in a blender until very smooth.

2. Pour the smoothie into a bowl and top with raspberries, the remaining 2 tablespoons almonds and honey.

Chai Chia Pudding

Ingredients

- ½ cup unsweetened almond milk or other nondairy milk

- 2 tablespoons chia seeds

- 2 teaspoons pure maple syrup

- ¼ teaspoon vanilla extract

- ¼ teaspoon ground cinnamon

- Pinch of ground cardamom

- Pinch of ground cloves

- ½ cup sliced banana, divided

- 1 tablespoon chopped unsalted roasted pistachios, divided

Directions

1. Stir almond milk (or other nondairy milk beverage), chia, maple syrup, vanilla, cinnamon, cardamom and cloves together in a small bowl. Cover and refrigerate for at least 8 hours and up to 3 days.

2. When ready to serve, stir well. Spoon about half the pudding into a serving glass (or bowl) and top

with half the banana and pistachios. Add the rest of the pudding and top with the remaining banana and pistachios.

Tips

To make ahead: Refrigerate pudding (Step 1) for up to 3 days. Finish with Step 2 just before serving.

Cherry Smoothie

Ingredients

- ½ cup oat milk

- 1 tablespoon almond butter

- 1 teaspoon cocoa powder

- ½ teaspoon vanilla extract

- 1 cup frozen dark sweet cherries

- 1 tablespoon brown sugar (Optional)

Directions

1. Add oat milk, almond butter, cocoa, vanilla, cherries and sugar (if using) to a blender. Blend until smooth.

Blueberry Almond Chia Pudding

Ingredients

- ½ cup unsweetened almond milk or other nondairy milk beverage

- 2 tablespoons chia seeds

- 2 teaspoons pure maple syrup

- ⅛ teaspoon almond extract

- ½ cup fresh blueberries, divided

- 1 tablespoon toasted slivered almonds, divided

Directions

1. Stir together almond milk (or other nondairy milk beverage), chia, maple syrup and almond extract in a small bowl. Cover and refrigerate for at least 8 hours and up to 3 days.

2. When ready to serve, stir the pudding well. Spoon about half the pudding into a serving glass (or bowl) and top with half the blueberries and almonds. Add the rest of the pudding and top with the remaining blueberries and almonds.

Tips

To make ahead: Refrigerate pudding (Step 1) for up to 3 days. Finish with Step 2 just before serving.

Peanut Butter-Banana English Muffin

Ingredients

- 1 whole-wheat English muffin, toasted

- 1 tablespoon peanut butter

- ½ banana, sliced

- Pinch of ground cinnamon

Directions

1. Top English muffin with peanut butter, banana and cinnamon.

"Egg in a Hole" Peppers with Avocado Salsa

Ingredients

- 2 bell peppers, any color

- 1 avocado, diced

- ½ cup diced red onion

- 1 jalapeño pepper, minced

- ½ cup chopped fresh cilantro, plus more for garnish

- 2 tomatoes, seeded and diced

- Juice of 1 lime

- ¾ teaspoon salt, divided

- 2 teaspoons olive oil, divided

- 8 large eggs

- ¼ teaspoon ground pepper, divided

Directions

1. Slice tops and bottoms off bell peppers and finely dice. Remove and discard seeds and membranes. Slice each pepper into four 1/2-inch-thick rings.

2. Combine the diced pepper with avocado, onion, jalapeño, cilantro, tomatoes, lime juice, and 1/2 teaspoon salt in a medium bowl.

3. Heat 1 teaspoon oil in a large nonstick skillet over medium heat. Add 4 bell pepper rings, then crack 1 egg into the middle of each ring. Season with 1/8 teaspoon each salt and pepper. Cook until the whites are mostly set but the yolks are still

runny, 2 to 3 minutes. Gently flip and cook 1 minute more for runny yolks, 1 1/2 to 2 minutes more for firmer yolks. Transfer to serving plates and repeat with the remaining pepper rings and eggs.

4. Serve with the avocado salsa and garnish with additional cilantro, if desired.

Everything Bagel Avocado Toast

Ingredients

- ¼ medium avocado, mashed

- 1 slice whole-grain bread, toasted

- 2 teaspoons everything bagel seasoning

- Pinch of flaky sea salt (such as Maldon)

Directions

1. Spread avocado on toast. Top with seasoning and salt.

Berry-Almond Smoothie Bowl

Ingredients

- ⅔ cup frozen raspberries

- ½ cup frozen sliced banana

- ½ cup plain unsweetened almond milk

- 5 tablespoons sliced almonds, divided

- ¼ teaspoon ground cinnamon

- ⅛ teaspoon ground cardamom

- ⅛ teaspoon vanilla extract

- ¼ cup blueberries

- 1 tablespoon unsweetened coconut flakes

Directions

1. Blend raspberries, banana, almond milk, 3 tablespoons almonds, cinnamon, cardamom and vanilla in a blender until very smooth.

2. Pour the smoothie into a bowl and top with blueberries, the remaining 2 tablespoons almonds and coconut.

Apple Cinnamon Chia Pudding

Ingredients

- ½ cup unsweetened almond milk or other nondairy milk

- 2 tablespoons chia seeds

- 2 teaspoons pure maple syrup

- ¼ teaspoon vanilla extract

- ¼ teaspoon ground cinnamon

- ½ cup diced apple, divided

- 1 tablespoon chopped toasted pecans, divided

Directions

1. Stir almond milk (or other nondairy milk), chia, maple syrup, vanilla and cinnamon together in a small bowl. Cover and refrigerate for at least 8 hours and up to 3 days.

2. When ready to serve, stir well. Spoon about half the pudding into a serving glass (or bowl) and top with half the apple and pecans. Add the rest of the pudding and top with the remaining apple and pecans.

Tips

To make ahead: Refrigerate pudding (Step 1) for up to 3 days. Finish with Step 2 just before serving.

Jason Mraz's Avocado Green Smoothie

Ingredients

• 1 ¼ cups cold unsweetened almond milk or coconut milk beverage

• 1 ripe avocado

- 1 ripe banana

- 1 sweet apple, such as Honeycrisp, sliced

- ½ large or 1 small stalk celery, chopped

- 2 cups lightly packed kale leaves or spinach

- 1 1-inch piece peeled fresh ginger

- 8 ice cubes

Directions

1. Blend milk beverage, avocado, banana, apple, celery, kale (or spinach), ginger and ice in a blender until very smooth.

Cocoa-Chia Pudding with Raspberries

Ingredients

- ½ cup unsweetened almond milk or other nondairy milk

- 2 tablespoons chia seeds

- 2 teaspoons pure maple syrup

- ½ teaspoon unsweetened cocoa powder

- ¼ teaspoon vanilla extract

- ½ cup fresh raspberries, divided

- 1 tablespoon toasted sliced almonds, divided

Directions

1. Stir almond milk (or other nondairy milk), chia seeds, maple syrup, cocoa powder and vanilla together in a small bowl. Cover and refrigerate for at least 8 hours and up to 3 days.

2. When ready to serve, stir well. Spoon about half the pudding into a serving glass (or bowl) and top with half the raspberries and almonds. Add the rest of the pudding and top with the remaining raspberries and almonds.

Chapter 4: Recommended Kid-Friendly Lunch Recipes

Spicy Chicken

Ingredients

1 whole fryer chicken, approximately 4 lbs.

3 egg whites

1 0.4-ounce packet ranch-style salad dressing mix

1/2 tsp. ground black pepper

3/4 cup dry unseasoned bread crumbs

Cooking spray

1 Tbsp. corn oil

Instructions

Preheat oven to 375 degrees. Cut the chicken into 10 pieces, as equal as you can make them. Remove the skin and fat. Rinse the skinned chicken pieces under water and lay on paper towels to drain. Place the egg whites in a large bowl and mix well with a wire whisk. In a large zip-top plastic bag, combine the salad dressing mix, pepper and bread crumbs. Dip each piece of chicken in the egg whites to coat it. Then place several pieces of chicken at a time into the bag of seasonings and shake until they are coated. Coat a baking sheet with the cooking spray. Set the seasoning-coated chicken on the baking sheet and sprinkle with the remaining seasoned crumbs. Spray the chicken with the cooking spray to give it a crunchy texture when baked. Bake for 40 minutes in the preheated oven. Then brush the chicken pieces with the tablespoon of corn oil. Continue baking the chicken 10 minutes longer or until it is not pink. Serve 1 piece of chicken as a portion.

1 serving = 1/2 starch + 3 meat exchanges or 7 grams of carbohydrate

Buffalo Chicken Bites

Ingredients

Cooking spray

1 pound chicken breasts, cooked & cut into bite-size chunks

1/2 cup Red Hot sauce

3 Tbsp. melted, reduced-calorie margarine

2 tsp. dried parsley

1/4 tsp. garlic powder

Celery sticks

Reduced-fat salad dressing

Instructions

Preheat oven to 350 degrees. Coat a baking dish with cooking spray and place chicken bites in the dish. In a bowl, combine Red Hot sauce, margarine, parsley and garlic powder. Pour evenly over chicken. Bake for 20 minutes. Put a toothpick in each piece of chicken and place on serving tray. Serve with celery sticks and salad dressing. Serving size would be 7 pieces of chicken.

1 serving = 3 meat exchanges or 1 gram of carbohydrate

Sausage Cheese Balls

Ingredients

2 pounds sausage, uncooked

1-1/2 cups all-purpose baking/biscuit mix

4 cups shredded cheddar cheese

1/2 cup finely chopped onion

1/2 cup finely chopped celery

1/2 tsp. garlic powder

Instructions

Preheat oven to 375 degrees. Mix all Ingredients and form into 1-inch balls. Bake 15 minutes on ungreased cookie sheet until golden brown. Makes 6 dozen.

1 serving = 2 balls = 1 meat + 1 fat exchange or 4 grams of carbohydrate

Steak Fajitas

Ingredients

3 Tbsp. chili powder

1 tsp. ground cumin

1/2 tsp. salt

1/4 tsp. ground cayenne pepper

1-3/4 pounds steak

2 large red onions, sliced

1 Tbsp. olive oil

8 12-inch low-fat tortillas

Instructions

In a cup, mix chili powder, cumin, salt and ground pepper. Rub steak with 2 Tbsp. chili-powder mixture. Place steak on a plate; set aside. In large bowl, toss onion slices with oil and remaining chili-powder mixture. Layer two 24 x 18-inch sheets of heavy-duty foil to make a double thickness. Place onion mixture on center of foil. Bring short ends of foil up and over onions and fold several times to seal well. Fold remaining sides of foil several times to seal in juices. Place foil packed on grill over medium heat. Cook onions 20 minutes of until tender, turning packet over once during cooking. Place steak on grill with onions; cook steak 10-15 minutes, depending on thickness of steak for medium doneness, turning steak over once. Transfer steak to cutting board; let stand 10 minutes to allow juices to set for easier slicing. Transfer onions to a bowl to keep warm. Meanwhile, wrap tortillas in foil; heat near edge of grill over low heat until warm. To serve, thinly slice steak. Place sliced steak and onions on warm tortillas and roll up to eat. Garnish as desired. Makes 8 servings.

1 serving = 1 starch + 2 vegetables + 3 meat exchanges or 24 grams of carbohydrate

Cheesesteak Sandwiches

Ingredients

1/2 cup red wine vinegar

1 Tbsp. olive oil

1/2 tsp. salt

1/2 tsp. coarsely ground black pepper

3 garlic cloves, crushed with garlic press

3 medium red or green peppers, cleaned & cut lengthwise into quarters

2 medium red onions, cut into 1/2? thick slices

12 ounce beef top round steak, 1? thick

4 ounces provolone cheese, shredded

4 hero rolls, split horizontally

Instructions

In a small bowl mix vinegar, olive oil, salt, pepper and garlic. Place peppers and onions in large self-sealing plastic bag and the steak in another. Add 2 tablespoons of vinegar mixture to bag with the vegetables and 1/4 cup mixture to bag with the steak. Save remaining mixture. Seal bags, pressing out excess air. Marinate for 15 minutes at room temperature. Then remove steak and vegetables from bags and place on grill over medium heat for 15–20 minutes or until desired doneness. Cook vegetables on grill with steak until browned or just tender. Let steak stand for 10 minutes for easier slicing. Transfer steak and vegetables to cutting board. Meanwhile, sprinkle cheese over cut rolls. Place rolls on grill, cheese side up, and cook over medium heat 3 minutes or until cheese melts. Transfer to platter. To serve, thinly slice steak, cut peppers into strips and separate onion slices into rings. Pile steak, peppers and onions over melted cheese on bottom halves of rolls. Drizzle with reserved vinegar mixture and replace top halves of rolls, cheese side down. Makes 4 sandwiches.

1 sandwich = 4 starch + 6 meat exchanges or 61 grams of carbohydrate

Taco Bundles

Ingredients

8 ounces ground beef

4 ounces tomato sauce, canned

1/2 cup cheddar cheese, shredded

1 Tbsp. taco seasoning mix

1 can (8) refrigerated crescent rolls

Non-stick cooking spray

Instructions

Preheat oven to 375 degrees. Brown ground beef until it is no longer pink; drain grease. Stir in seasoning mix and tomato sauce; set aside. Separate crescent rolls into 4 large rectangles. Pinch seams together. On lightly floured board, roll rectangles a little wider. Stir shredded cheese into ground beef mixture. Divide meat into 4 equal portions. Place on portion of meat on one side of each rectangle. Apply a little bit of water to edge of each rectangle and fold in half. Use fork to seal edges together. Place bundles on cookie sheet that has been lined with foil and sprayed with cooking spray. Bake in oven for 15–20 minutes or until golden brown.

1 serving = 1 bundle = 2 starch + 2 meat + 3 fat exchanges or 26 grams of carbohydrate

Chicken Chili

Ingredients

2 Tbsp. corn oil

1-1/2 pound boneless, skinless chicken breasts, cut into 1" cubes

1 small onion, chopped

1 medium green bell pepper, chopped

1/2 cup chicken broth

1-41/2 ounce can red kidney beans, undrained

1-41/2 ounce can diced tomatoes

1 Tbsp. ground chili powder

1-1/2 tsp. garlic salt

1 tsp. ground cumin

1 tsp. oregano or cilantro leaves

Instructions

Heat oil in Dutch oven or large saucepan over medium-high heat. Add chicken, onion and bell pepper; saute 8–10 minutes. Stir in remaining Ingredients. Bring to a boil. Simmer 15 minutes. Makes 6 cups.

1 serving = 1 cup = 1 starch + 4 meat + 1 fat exchange or 18 grams of carbohydrate

Chipotle-Lime Cauliflower Taco Bowls

Ingredients

- ¼ cup lime juice (from about 2 limes)

- 1-2 tablespoons chopped chipotles in adobo sauce (see Tip)

- 1 tablespoon honey

- 2 cloves garlic

- ½ teaspoon salt

- 1 small head cauliflower, cut into bite-size pieces

- 1 small red onion, halved and thinly sliced

- 2 cups cooked quinoa, cooled

- 1 cup no-salt-added canned black beans, rinsed

- ½ cup crumbled queso fresco

- 1 cup shredded red cabbage

- 1 medium avocado

- 1 lime, cut into 4 wedges (Optional)

Directions

1. Preheat oven to 450°F. Line a large rimmed baking sheet with foil.

2. Combine lime juice, chipotles to taste, honey, garlic and salt in a blender. Process until mostly smooth. Place cauliflower in a large bowl; add the

sauce and stir to coat. Transfer to the prepared baking sheet. Sprinkle onion over the cauliflower. Roast, stirring once, until the cauliflower is tender and browned in spots, 18 to 20 minutes; set aside to cool.

3. Divide quinoa among 4 single-serving lidded containers (1/2 cup each). Top each with one-fourth of the cauliflower mixture, 1/4 cup black beans and 2 tablespoons cheese. Seal the containers and refrigerate for up to 4 days.

4. To reheat 1 container, vent the lid and microwave on High until steaming, 2 1/2 to 3 minutes. Top with 1/4 cup cabbage and 1/4 avocado (sliced). Serve with a lime wedge, if desired.

Tip

Look for small cans of smoked chipotle peppers in adobo sauce near other Mexican Ingredients in well-stocked supermarkets. Once opened, refrigerate for up to 2 weeks or freeze for up to 6 months.

Avocado, Tomato & Chicken Sandwich

Ingredients

- 2 slices multigrain bread

- ¼ ripe avocado

- 3 ounces cooked boneless, skinless chicken breast, sliced (see Tip)

- 2 slices tomato

Directions

1. Toast bread. Mash avocado with a fork and spread onto one piece of toast. Top with chicken, tomato and the second piece of toast.

Tips

Tip: If you don't have cooked chicken, you can poach it to use in a recipe. Place boneless, skinless chicken breasts in a skillet or saucepan. Add lightly salted water to cover and bring to a boil. Cover, reduce heat to a simmer and cook until no longer pink in the middle, 10 to 15 minutes, depending on size. (Eight ounces raw boneless, skinless chicken breast yields about 1 cup sliced, diced or shredded cooked chicken.)

Spaghetti Squash with Roasted Tomatoes, Beans & Almond Pesto

Ingredients

Almond Pesto

- 2 cups fresh basil leaves

- 1 cup fresh parsley leaves

- ½ cup grated Parmesan cheese

- ⅓ cup whole raw almonds

- 1 clove garlic

- 1 ½ tablespoons red-wine vinegar

- ¼ teaspoon kosher salt

- ¼ teaspoon ground pepper

- ¼ cup extra-virgin olive oil

- ¼ cup water

Spaghetti Squash & Vegetables

- 1 3-pound spaghetti squash

- ¼ cup water

- 2 pints grape tomatoes, halved

- 1 tablespoon extra-virgin olive oil

- ¼ teaspoon kosher salt

- ¼ teaspoon ground pepper

- 1 cup canned cannellini beans, rinsed

Directions

1. To prepare pesto: Pulse basil, parsley, Parmesan, almonds, garlic, vinegar and 1/4 teaspoon each salt and pepper in a food processor until coarsely chopped, scraping down the sides. With the motor running, add 1/4 cup oil; process until well combined.

2. Add water to the pesto in the food processor; pulse to combine.

3. To prepare squash & vegetables: Preheat oven to 400 degrees F. Line a rimmed baking sheet with foil.

4. Halve squash lengthwise and scoop out the seeds. Place cut-side down in a microwave-safe dish and add water. Microwave on High until the flesh can be easily scraped with a fork, about 15 minutes.

5. Meanwhile, toss tomatoes with oil, salt and pepper in a large bowl. Transfer to the prepared baking sheet. Roast until soft and wrinkled, 10 to 12 minutes. Remove from the oven. Add beans and stir to combine.

6. Scrape the squash flesh into the bowl and divide among 4 plates. Top each portion with some of the tomato-bean mixture and about 3 tablespoons pesto sauce.

Tips

To make ahead: Refrigerate pesto (Step 1) for up to 5 days.

Tips: Turn leftovers into a pesto-turkey sandwich for lunch: Spread 1 1/2 Tbsp. leftover pesto on 2 slices toasted whole-wheat bread. Top with 3 oz.

sliced deli turkey, 2 lettuce leaves and 2 tomato slices.

Chicken, Spinach & Feta Wraps

Ingredients

• 1/2 cup whole-milk plain strained (Greek-style) yogurt

• 1/4 cup crumbled feta cheese

• 2 tablespoons finely chopped oil-packed sun-dried tomatoes

• 1 tablespoon dried oregano

• 2 teaspoons grated lemon zest

• 1/2 teaspoon garlic powder

- 1/2 teaspoon crushed red pepper

- 1/4 teaspoon ground pepper

- 2 cups shredded rotisserie chicken

- 4 (10-inch) whole wheat tortillas

- 4 cups packed fresh baby spinach

Directions

1. Stir yogurt, feta, sun-dried tomatoes, oregano, lemon zest, garlic powder, crushed red pepper and pepper together in a large bowl; mash with a fork until mostly smooth, about 1 minute. (Alternatively, process in a blender until creamy, 30 to 45 seconds.) Fold in chicken, coating with the yogurt mixture.

2. Arrange tortillas on a work surface. Place 1 cup spinach and about 1/2 cup chicken mixture in a line in the center of each tortilla. Fold bottom edge and side edges over the filling; roll up burrito-style. Cut into halves before serving.

Cucumber Sandwich with Cotija & Lime

Ingredients

• 2 tablespoons low-fat plain strained yogurt, such as Greek-style

• 1 ½ tablespoons crumbled cotija cheese

• 1 tablespoon finely chopped fresh cilantro

• ½ teaspoon lime zest

• ⅛ teaspoon ground pepper

- 1 multigrain sandwich thin, split and lightly toasted

- ⅓ cup thinly sliced English cucumber

- ¼ cup arugula or mixed salad greens

Directions

1. Stir yogurt, cotija, cilantro, lime zest and pepper together in a small bowl.

2. Spread the mixture evenly on both halves of sandwich thin. Top one half with cucumber slices and arugula (or mixed salad greens). Place the other half on top. Cut the sandwich in half and serve.

Chickpea & Roasted Red Pepper Lettuce Wraps with Tahini Dressing

Ingredients

- ¼ cup tahini

- ¼ cup extra-virgin olive oil

- 1 teaspoon lemon zest

- ¼ cup lemon juice (from 2 lemons)

- 1 ½ teaspoons pure maple syrup

- ¾ teaspoon kosher salt

- ½ teaspoon paprika

- 2 (15 ounce) cans no-salt-added chickpeas, rinsed

- ½ cup sliced jarred roasted red peppers, drained

- ½ cup thinly sliced shallots

- 12 large Bibb lettuce leaves

- ¼ cup toasted almonds, chopped

- 2 tablespoons chopped fresh parsley

Directions

1. Whisk tahini, oil, lemon zest, lemon juice, maple syrup, salt and paprika in a large bowl. Add chickpeas, peppers and shallots. Toss to coat.

2. Divide the mixture among lettuce leaves (about 1/3 cup each). Top with almonds and parsley. Wrap the lettuce leaves around the filling and serve.

Lentil Burgers

Ingredients

- 1 large clove garlic, peeled

- 1/4 teaspoon kosher salt

- ½ cup walnuts, toasted (see Tips)

- 2 slices whole-wheat sandwich bread, crusts removed, torn into pieces

- 1 tablespoon chopped fresh marjoram or 1 teaspoon dried

- ¼ teaspoon freshly ground pepper

- 1 1/2 cups cooked or canned (rinsed) lentils (see Tips)

- 2 teaspoons Worcestershire sauce, vegetarian (see Note) or regular

- 3 teaspoons canola oil, divided

- 4 whole-wheat hamburger buns, toasted

- 4 pieces leaf lettuce

- 4 slices tomato or jarred roasted red pepper

- 4 thin slices red onion

Directions

1. Coarsely chop garlic; sprinkle with salt and mash to a paste with the side of the knife. Coarsely chop walnuts in a food processor. Add bread, marjoram, pepper and the garlic paste; process until coarse crumbs form. Add lentils and Worcestershire; process until the mixture just

comes together in a mass. Form into four 3-inch patties (about 1/3 cup each).

2. Heat 2 teaspoons oil in a large nonstick skillet over medium heat. Cook the patties until browned on the bottom, 2 to 4 minutes. Carefully turn over; reduce heat to medium-low. Drizzle the remaining 1 teaspoon oil around the burgers and cook until browned on the other side and heated through, 4 to 6 minutes more. Serve on buns with lettuce, tomato (or red pepper) and onion.

Tips

Make Ahead Tip: Prepare through Step 1, tightly wrap in plastic and refrigerate for up to 1 day or freeze for up to 3 months. If frozen, let defrost in the refrigerator before cooking.

Tips:

To toast nuts: Spread whole nuts on a baking sheet and bake at 350°F, stirring once, until fragrant, 7 to 9 minutes. Toast chopped, small or sliced nuts in a small dry skillet over medium-low heat, stirring constantly, until fragrant and lightly browned, 2 to 4 minutes.

To cook lentils: Place in a saucepan, cover with at least 1 inch of water, bring to a simmer and cook until just tender, 15 to 30 minutes, depending on the type of lentil. Drain and rinse with cold water. 1 cup dry lentils = about 2 1/2 cups cooked. Or use canned lentils: 15-ounce can = 1 1/2 cups. Rinse canned lentils before cooking with them to reduce the sodium by about 35%.

Note: Regular Worcestershire sauce contains anchovies and is not vegetarian. Look for vegetarian Worcestershire--flavored with molasses, soy sauce and vinegar--near other bottled sauces in natural foods stores or in the natural foods section of well-stocked supermarkets.

Storage smarts: For long-term freezer storage, wrap your food in a layer of plastic wrap followed by a layer of foil. The plastic will help prevent freezer burn while the foil will help keep off-odors from seeping into the food.

Pesto Chicken & Cannellini Bean Soup

Ingredients

- 2 tablespoons extra-virgin olive oil

- 1 cup chopped onion

- 2 large cloves garlic, minced

- 1 tablespoon chopped fresh oregano or 1 teaspoon dried

- 1 tablespoon chopped fresh marjoram or 1 teaspoon dried

- 8 cups low-sodium chicken broth

- 2 pounds bone-in chicken breasts, skin removed

- 3 cups sliced fennel

- 3 cups broccolini (1-inch pieces; about 1 bunch)

- 2 cups chopped tomatoes

- 1 15-ounce can cannellini beans, rinsed

- 1 ¼ teaspoons salt

- ½ teaspoon ground pepper

- ¼ cup prepared pesto

Directions

1. Heat oil in a large pot over medium heat. Add onion and garlic and cook, stirring occasionally, until softened, 2 to 3 minutes. Add oregano and marjoram; cook, stirring, for 1 minute. Add broth and chicken. Cover, increase heat to high and bring to a simmer. Uncover and cook, turning the chicken occasionally, until an instant-read thermometer inserted into the thickest part without touching bone registers 165 degrees F, 20 to 22 minutes. Skim any foam from the surface as the chicken cooks. Transfer the chicken to a clean

cutting board. When cool enough to handle, remove the meat from the bones and shred.

2. Meanwhile, add fennel, broccolini and tomatoes to the pot; return to a simmer. Cook until the vegetables are tender, 4 to 10 minutes. Stir in the shredded chicken, beans, salt and pepper and cook until heated through, about 3 minutes more. Remove from heat and stir in pesto.

Tips

To make ahead: Cover and refrigerate, without the pesto, for up to 3 days. To serve, reheat and then stir in pesto.

Spicy Slaw Bowls with Shrimp & Edamame

Ingredients

- Spicy Cabbage Slaw

- 2 cups frozen shelled edamame, thawed

- 1 medium avocado, diced

- ½ medium lime, juiced

- 12 ounces peeled cooked shrimp

Directions

1. Prepare Spicy Cabbage Slaw. Add edamame; toss and set aside.

2. Toss avocado with lime juice in a small bowl.

3. Divide the slaw mixture among 4 containers. Top each with 1/4 of the shrimp (about 3 ounces) and 1/4 of the avocado. Cover and refrigerate until ready to eat.

Mason Jar Power Salad with Chickpeas & Tuna

Ingredients

- 3 cups bite-sized pieces chopped kale

- 2 tablespoons honey-mustard vinaigrette

- 1 2.5-ounce pouch tuna in water

- ½ cup rinsed canned chickpeas

- 1 carrot, peeled and shredded

Directions

1. Toss kale and dressing in a bowl, then tranfer to a 1-quart mason jar. Top with tuna, chickpeas and carrot. Screw lid onto the jar and refrigerate for up to 2 days.

2. To serve, empty the jar contents into a bowl and toss to combine the salad Ingredients with the dressed kale.

Egg Salad English-Muffin Sandwich

Ingredients

• 1 whole-wheat English muffin, split

• 1 teaspoon olive oil

• 2 medium carrots with tops (see Tips)

• 2 large hard-boiled eggs (see Tips)

• 1 tablespoon plus 1 tsp. mayonnaise

• 1 large romaine lettuce leaf, shredded

Directions

1. Preheat a grill pan or skillet (not nonstick) over medium-high heat. Brush cut sides of English muffin halves with oil. Grill the muffins until both sides are lightly browned, 1 to 2 minutes per side.

2. Peel carrots, if desired; cut into sticks. Chop 1 Tbsp. of the carrot tops.

3. Dice hard-boiled eggs and place in a small bowl. Add mayonnaise and the chopped carrot tops; stir until combined. Divide lettuce between the grilled muffin halves; top with the egg salad. Serve the carrots on the side.

Tip

If you can't find carrots with tops, use ½ tsp. dried dill or 1 minced fresh scallion in place of the carrot leaves in Step 2.

To reduce saturated fat, use a combination of 1 large hard-boiled egg and the whites from 2 large hard-boiled eggs. Reserve the cooked egg yolks for another purpose, such as topping a green salad.

Anti-Inflammatory Beet & Avocado Wrap

Ingredients

- 1 tablespoon lemon juice

- 1 tablespoon tahini

- 1 teaspoon extra-virgin olive oil

- ⅛ teaspoon kosher salt

- ⅛ teaspoon ground pepper

- ½ cup julienned red beets

- 1 ½ tablespoons hummus

- 1 (8 inch) whole-wheat tortilla

- 2 leaves butter lettuce

- ½ medium avocado, sliced

Directions

1. Whisk lemon juice, tahini, oil, salt and pepper together in a medium bowl. Add beets; toss to coat.

2. Spread hummus evenly over 1 side of tortilla. Place lettuce over hummus; top with beet mixture and avocado slices. Roll up burrito-style; slice in half.

Quinoa Deli Salad

Ingredients

- 3 cups coarsely chopped Bibb, Boston, or butterhead lettuce

- ¼ cup thinly sliced red bell pepper

- 2 tablespoons red-wine vinaigrette, divided (see Tip)

- ¼ cup cooked quinoa

- ½ cup canned low-sodium chickpeas, rinsed

- ¼ cup drained canned artichoke hearts, quartered

- 1 slice low-sodium deli ham, diced (1 oz.)

- 2 tablespoons shredded low-moisture, part-skim mozzarella cheese (1/2 oz.)

Directions

1. Toss lettuce and pepper with 1 Tbsp. plus 1 tsp. vinaigrette and place on a 9-inch plate.

2. Toss quinoa and chickpeas with the remaining 2 tsp. vinaigrette and place on top of the lettuce and pepper. Top with artichokes, ham, and mozzarella.

Tips

Tip: To make a quick homemade red-wine vinaigrette, whisk 2 Tbsp. red-wine vinegar with 1/8 tsp. each salt and pepper. Slowly whisk in 1/4 cup extra-virgin olive oil until blended. Extra dressing will keep, covered, in the refrigerator, for up to 5 days. Bring to room temperature before using.

3-Ingredient Salmon & Veggie Sandwich

Ingredients

• 1 3-ounce piece baguette or crusty roll, split in half

• 1/2 cup chopped grilled or roasted vegetables

• 2 ounces cooked salmon, flaked (about 1/4 cup)

Directions

1. Scoop out soft insides from top half of baguette (or roll). Arrange vegetables and salmon on bottom half; top with the hollowed-out piece.

Mixed Greens with Lentils & Sliced Apple

Ingredients

- 1 ½ cups mixed salad greens

- ½ cup cooked lentils

- 1 apple, cored and sliced, divided

- 1 ½ tablespoons crumbled feta cheese

- 1 tablespoon red-wine vinegar

- 2 teaspoons extra-virgin olive oil

Directions

1. Top greens with lentils, about half the apple slices and the feta. Drizzle with vinegar and oil. Serve with the remaining apple slices on the side.

Shredded Chicken & Avocado Nacho Salad

Ingredients

- ¾ cup pico de gallo, divided

- 4 teaspoons extra-virgin olive oil

- 6 cups coarsely chopped iceberg lettuce

- 2 cups shredded skinless, boneless rotisserie chicken breast

- 2 ripe peeled avocados, sliced

- 2 ounces multigrain tortilla chips (about 20 chips)

- ¼ teaspoon freshly ground black pepper

Directions

1. Combine 1/2 cup pico de gallo and oil in a mini food processor; process until smooth. Set aside.

2. Spread lettuce evenly over a large platter; top with chicken and avocado. Drizzle evenly with blended pico de gallo and remaining 1/4 cup pico de gallo. Sprinkle with tortilla chips and pepper.

Chapter 5: Recommended Kid-Friendly Dinner Recipes

Vegetable Soup

Ingredients

8 ounces ground chuck

7 cups tomatoes, peeled and chopped

4 cups water

14.5 ounce can cut green beans, drained and rinsed

15 ounce can peas, drained and rinsed

15.25 ounce can corn, drained and rinsed

2 carrots, peeled and chopped

3 potatoes, peeled and diced

1 medium onion, diced

1/4 cup dry rice

1/8 tsp. black pepper

1/8 tsp. red pepper flakes

1/2 tsp. salt

1/2 tsp. garlic powder

Instructions

Place ground chuck in 2-gallon stockpot and brown over medium heat. Remove meat and drain it well. Clean meat drippings from stockpot. Return meat to stockpot and add tomatoes and water. Bring to a simmer and cook 20 minutes or until the tomatoes are soft and a juicy broth is created. Add the remaining Ingredients, cover and continue cooking an additional 60 minutes. Makes 14 8-ounce servings.

1 serving = 1 starch + 1 vegetable + 1 meat exchange or 23 grams of carbohydrate

Curried Turkey and Biscuits

Ingredients

5 biscuits, prepared from refrigerator dough

1 Tbsp. margarine

1 red onion, sliced

1/2 cup mushrooms

1 10.5 ounce can of cream of mushroom soup, condensed

1 tsp. curry powder

1/2 cup sour cream

2-1/2 cups turkey, cubed

1/4 cup parsley, chopped

Instructions

Prepare biscuits according to package directions. In a large frying pan over medium heat, melt margarine and saute onions and sliced mushrooms. Stir in soup, curry powder and sour cream to make a smooth sauce. Add turkey chunks and chopped parsley. Continue to simmer until completely heated. Serve over biscuits. Makes 5 servings.

1 serving = 2 starch + 4 meat + 3 fat exchanges or 28 grams of carbohydrate

Skillet Dinner

Ingredients

4 medium potatoes, sliced 1/4? thick & microwaved 6–10 minutes until tender

16 ounces london broil, thinly sliced

1 Tbsp. garlic powder

2 Tbsp. olive oil

1 green bell pepper, cut into thin strips

Instructions

While potatoes cook in microwave, toss beef with garlic pepper and heat oil in large skillet over high heat. Add beef to skillet and toss 3 minutes. Remove beef and add green pepper to skill; toss 3 minutes. Add potatoes; saute 5 minutes with peppers. Add beef and toss until heated through. Makes 5 servings.

1 serving = 3 starch + 3 meat + 2 fat exchanges or 41 grams of carbohydrate

Ham & Cheese Casserole

Ingredients

2 cups fresh or frozen broccoli flowerets, thawed

1-1/2 cups reduced fat cheddar cheese, shredded

1-1/2 cups coarsely chopped ham

1-1/2 cups rotini pasta, cooked & drained

1/2 cup light Miracle Whip dressing

1/2 green or red pepper, chopped

1/4 cup 2% milk

Instructions

Preheat oven to 350 degrees. Mix all Ingredients except 1/2 cup of the cheese. Spoon into 1-1/2-quart casserole dish. Sprinkle top with remaining 1/2 cup cheese. Bake for 30 minutes or until thoroughly heated. Makes 6 servings.

1 serving = 1 starch + 2 meat + 1 fat exchange or 13 grams of carbohydrate

Pasta Skillet Dinner

Ingredients

1 pound Lean ground beef

3 cups mostacciolli, uncooked

1 jar (28 ounces) spaghetti sauce

8 ounces mozzarella cheese, shredded

1/4 cup parmesan cheese, grated

Instructions

Brown meat in large skillet and drain fat. Add 2-1/2 cups water and bring to a boil. Reduce heat and stir in pasta. Cover skillet and simmer for 15 minutes or until pasta is tender. Stir in spaghetti sauce and 1 cup of mozzarella cheese. Sprinkle with remaining cheeses and cover. Cook 3 minutes or until cheese is melted. Makes 6 servings.

1 serving = 3 starch + 3 meat + 3 fat exchanges or 40 grams of carbohydrate

Tex Mex Chicken Wings

Ingredients

2-1/2 pounds chicken wings, separated at joints and tips discarded

1 cup barbecue sauce

1 Tbsp. chili powder

1 tsp. garlic powder

Instructions

Preheat oven to 450 degrees. Place chicken in 15" x 10" x 1" baking pan lined with foil. Bake at 450 degrees for 35 minutes. Drain grease. Mix remaining three Ingredients. Brush wings with barbecue sauce mixture and bake an additional 10 minutes. Makes 12 servings of about 4 wings each.

1 serving = 4 meat + 1 fruit exchange or 13 grams of carbohydrate

Chicken Quesadillas Recipe

Ingredients

- 2 teaspoons canola oil, divided

- 4 (10-inch) flour tortillas

- 2 cups shredded cooked rotisserie chicken, divided

• 2 cups shredded cheddar cheese, divided

Steps to Make It

1. Gather the Ingredients.

2. Heat 1 teaspoon of the oil in a large frying pan over medium heat.

3. While the pan is heating, assemble the quesadillas. Sprinkle 1/2 cup of chicken over half of each tortilla. Top with 1/2 cup of cheese.

4. Fold in half and place 1 quesadilla at a time in the skillet. Let it cook for 2 minutes until golden brown on one side.

5. Flip with tongs or a spatula and cook another 2 minutes until cheese is melted and the quesadilla is brown on the other side. Remove to a plate.

6. Repeat with remaining quesadillas. Then serve immediately. Enjoy!

Tip

• Serve these chicken quesadillas with tomato salsa, sour cream, and guacamole for a heartier version.

• If you're more in the mood for a casserole-type dish, try this chicken casserole with black beans, corn, and salsa recipe.

Recipe Variation

• These quesadillas can be made as is, or jazz them up by adding such Ingredients as: black beans, chopped onions, corn, tomatoes, cilantro, mushrooms, spinach, or jalapeños into the tortilla, putting them on in between the chicken and cheese. Come up with your own customized version and make this your own!

• Use a Mexican blended shredded cheese, pepper jack cheese, mozzarella cheese, or even havarti cheese. It all depends on what type of cheese you're in the mood for.

• If you prefer corn tortillas, feel free to use them, just allot the amount of **Ingredients** you put inside for the difference in size. You don't want to overfill and have it come out during cooking.

Easy Cheesy Baked Ziti Recipe

Ingredients

• 16 ounces ziti pasta

• 1 large egg

- 15 ounces ricotta cheese

- 1/2 teaspoon garlic powder

- 1/4 cup chopped fresh basil, optional

- 2 cups shredded mozzarella cheese, divided

- 4 1/2 cups store-bought or homemade spaghetti sauce, divided

- 1/2 cup grated Parmesan cheese

Steps to Make It

1. Gather the **Ingredients**. Preheat oven to 350 F.

2. Prepare pasta according to package directions for "al dente." Drain.

3. In a large bowl, beat egg. Add ricotta cheese, garlic powder, basil (if using), and 1 cup of the mozzarella. Mix well.

4. Add cooked pasta and 2 cups of the spaghetti sauce.

5. Pour 1 cup of the spaghetti sauce in a 9 x 13-inch pan.

6. Top with the ziti mixture. Top with the remaining sauce. Sprinkle remaining mozzarella and Parmesan cheese over the sauce.

7. Cover with foil and bake for 20 minutes.

8. Remove foil and bake another 10 to 20 minutes until golden brown and bubbly. Let the pasta rest 10 minutes before serving.

Maple-Dijon Pork Chops Recipe

Ingredients

- 4 bone-in pork rib chops, about 1-inch thick

- 2 tablespoons chopped fresh tarragon leaves, or flat-leaf parsley, for garnish

For Rub:

- 2 teaspoons sea salt

- 2 teaspoons onion powder

- 1 teaspoon marjoram

- 1/2 teaspoon freshly ground black pepper

- 1/4 teaspoon garlic powder

- 1/2 teaspoon herbes de Provence, optional

For Glaze:

- 1/2 cup real maple syrup

- 1/4 cup Dijon mustard

- 1 tablespoon olive oil

Steps to Make It

1. Gather the **Ingredients**.

2. Preheat the grill for high heat. In a small bowl, combine the maple syrup with Dijon mustard and olive oil. Set aside.

3. Combine salt, onion, and garlic powder, marjoram, pepper, and herbes de provence (if using) and evenly pat onto both sides of pork chops. Place onto grill and cook for 15 minutes, turning occasionally.

4. During the last 3 to 4 minutes of cooking, brush on maple glaze. Cook for 1 minute, turn and repeat the process. (Make sure to keep a close eye during this phase as the sugar content in maple syrup can cause flare-ups.)

5. Once chops are cooked through, remove from heat and place onto a platter. Let rest for 5 minutes and garnish with chopped tarragon or parsley leaves.

Tips

• When brushing the maple glaze on the pork chops, watch for grill flare-ups.

• After cooking, remember to let the pork chops rest for 5 minutes before serving. This will allow the juices to settle within the meat, allowing for a juicy and tender chop.

• Pork is cooked when it reaches an internal temperature of 145 F, which is the FDA-recommended minimum safe temperature for all pork cuts. Check with an instant-read thermometer to ensure the pork chops are cooked.

Electric Skillet Barbecue Chicken

Ingredients

• 1 teaspoon oil

• 3 pounds chicken pieces

• Kosher salt, to taste

• Freshly ground black pepper, to taste

- 16 ounces barbecue sauce

- 16 ounces orange soda

Steps to Make It

1. Preheat an electric skillet to 275 F. Add oil.

2. Season chicken on both sides with salt and pepper. When oil is hot, add chicken to the skillet. Brown for 2 minutes on the first side. Flip.

3. Add the barbecue sauce and orange soda.

4. Cook, basting occasionally, 35 to 40 minutes until chicken is cooked through.

Tip

For this recipe, you can use your favorite barbecue sauce, or opt to make one from scratch if you like.

You can experiment with Carolina or Memphis-style sauce, or opt for one with Jack Daniel's in it.

Variations

• This recipe calls for orange soda, but you could use cola instead if you prefer. The flavor will be slightly different.

• Feel free to use a combination of wings and drumsticks, or all wings, or all drumsticks.

How to Store and Freeze Electric Skillet Barbecue Chicken

• You can keep chicken, once cooked, wrapped in foil or in an airtight container in the fridge for three to four days. As a next-day leftover, it's especially good eaten cold in a salad, or tossed into a soup.

• Freeze the chicken, well-wrapped, for up to six months and defrost in the refrigerator. Gently reheat in the oven, or use cold and incorporate in tacos, soups, or salads.

Loaded Baked Potato Soup

Ingredients

• 8 to 10 slices bacon (diced, about 8 ounces)

• 4 tablespoons butter

• 1/2 cup celery (diced)

• 1 cup onion (diced)

• 8 green onions (thinly sliced)

• 1/3 cup all-purpose flour

- 3 cups chicken broth

- 2 cups half-and-half

- 2 to 3 pounds russet baking potatoes (baked, peeled, and diced)

- 1 teaspoon salt (or to taste)

- 1/4 teaspoon ground black pepper

- 8 ounces sharp cheddar cheese (shredded)

- 8 ounces sour cream

- Optional: sliced green onion for garnish

Steps to Make It

1. In a Dutch oven or large kettle over medium heat, cook the bacon until crisp. Remove bacon to

paper towels to drain and pour the bacon drippings into a cup.

2. Put 2 tablespoons of bacon drippings back into the pot along with the butter, chopped onion, and celery. Cook, stirring until vegetables are tender.

3. Stir in the sliced green onion and flour until blended. Cook, stirring, for 2 minutes.

4. Stir in chicken broth; cover and continue cooking, stirring frequently, until the mixture is thickened and vegetables are very tender.

5. Stir in half-and-half, diced potatoes, salt, pepper, and cheese. Continue cooking until cheese is melted.

6. Blend about half of the soup in batches until smooth.

7. Add the blended soup back to the pot and add sour cream.

8. Cook, stirring constantly until soup is hot.

9. Serve the soup garnished with bacon and extra sliced green onion if desired.

Instant Pot Beef Stew Recipe

Ingredients

- 2 pounds boneless beef chuck roast

- 1 teaspoon kosher salt, more to taste

- 1/2 teaspoon black pepper, more to taste

- 2 tablespoons canola oil, divided

- 1 medium yellow onion, coarsely chopped

- 4 cloves garlic, minced

- 1 tablespoon tomato paste

- 1/3 cup red wine

- 2 teaspoons fresh thyme leaves, or 1 teaspoon dried thyme

- 1 medium bay leaf

- 3/4 pound baby Yukon Gold potatoes

- 2 large carrots (about 1/2 pound), cut into 1 1/2-inch pieces

- 1 large parsnip (about 1/2 pound), cut into 1 1/2-inch pieces

- 2/3 cup beef broth

- 1 tablespoon cornstarch

- 1 tablespoon Worcestershire sauce

- 1 cup frozen green peas

Steps to Make It

1. Gather the **Ingredients**.

2. Place the beef on a cutting board and cut into 1-inch chunks, removing excess fat and gristle (some fat is good, but remove and discard any especially big pieces). Season all over with the salt and pepper.

3. Heat the Instant Pot on the sauté setting on high heat. Add 1 tablespoon of oil to coat the bottom of the pot. Add half of the beef in a single layer and let sear until browned, about 4 minutes. Use tongs to flip and brown the other side, about 3 minutes.

Remove the beef to a plate and repeat with the remaining beef. Set aside.

4. Add the remaining 1 tablespoon of oil to the Instant Pot. Add the onion and sauté, stirring occasionally, until beginning to turn translucent, about 2 minutes. Add the garlic and tomato paste; sauté just until fragrant, about 30 seconds.

5. Add the wine, thyme, and bay leaf. Scrape the bottom of the pot to dislodge any browned, stuck-on bits. Let simmer until the wine is reduced by half, about 1 minute.

6. Turn off the sauté function. Add the potatoes, carrots, parsnip, beef broth, and the browned beef along with any remaining juices to the pot. Stir to combine, then secure the lid. Cook at high pressure for 25 minutes. Use a natural release.

7. Once the pressure has released naturally, whisk together the cornstarch and Worcestershire sauce in a small bowl until no lumps remain.

8. Remove the bay leaf. Turn on the sauté function to high and add the peas. Once simmering, add the cornstarch mixture and stir. Simmer until thickened slightly, about 3 minutes.

9. Season with salt and pepper to taste. Serve warm.

Tips

• A whole cut of beef chuck is preferable to pre-cut stew meat. This is because stew meat often has excess fat and gristle still attached. Cutting up the beef yourself allows you to trim any unwanted bits and make sure the meat is uniform in size.

• Browning the meat before pressure cooking the stews adds tons of flavor. If you're short on time, you can skip this step and add the beef with the vegetables.

• This recipe calls for whole baby yellow potatoes. They should be between 1 inch and 1 1/2-inches across. You can use an equivalent amount of large potatoes cut into 1 1/2-inch cubes.

• A natural release ensures the stew is perfectly cooked and tender. This can take up to 30 minutes. If you're impatient, you can perform a quick release after a 15-minute natural release.

Recipe Variations

• A variety of vegetables work well in beef stew, just keep the ratio of vegetables to beef the same.

Try turnips, rutabaga, sweet potato, or butternut squash. For a simple beef stew, swap the parsnips for more potatoes and carrots.

• As the wine simmers in this recipe, all of the alcohol cooks off. If you don't have wine handy or prefer not to cook with it, replace it with more broth and add a tablespoon or two of balsamic vinegar along with the peas.

• If you don't have beef broth, chicken or vegetable broth can be used instead.

Vegetarian Pesto Pizza With Feta Cheese

Ingredients

• 1 (15-inch) pizza crust

• 1/2 cup pesto

- 6 ounces feta cheese, crumbled

- 1 (6-ounce) jar artichokes, drained and chopped, optional

- 1/3 cup sun-dried tomatoes, sliced, optional

- 1/2 cup Kalamata olives, chopped, optional

Steps to Make It

1. Gather the **Ingredients**.

2. Preheat oven to 400 F. Spread pesto over crust. Sprinkle on feta cheese. Add optional artichokes, sun-dried tomatoes, and olives to your liking.

3. Bake pizza for 15 minutes or until heated through and crust is browned. Slice and serve.

Enjoy this pizza with a fresh green salad for a lunch or dinner. Refrigerate any leftover pizza and reheat it later.

Frozen pre-made pizza crusts are readily available at the supermarket and are vegetarian. You may also find fresh pre-made crusts available at your grocery store.

If you have extra time, it is worthwhile to make your pizza dough. A whole wheat vegan pizza dough may add just the right touch. If you'd rather avoid gluten, you can make a vegan cornmeal pizza crust instead.

For that fresh yeast dough texture without having to let the dough rise, many grocery stores have pizza dough available in the refrigerated section next to the cheese and typical pizza toppings. You only need to roll it out, add the toppings, and bake it per their recommendations. Frozen pizza dough is available from Rhodes and other brands. You let it thaw before shaping the dough. Be sure to wear an apron to keep stray flour off your clothes, and you will have to clean up your rolling pin, board, and the inevitable dusting of flour on the countertop and floor.

Meatball Mac and Cheese

Ingredients

• Cooking spray

• 1 (16-ounce) box penne pasta

• Kosher salt, as needed

• 2 tablespoons unsalted butter

- 1 medium onion, finely chopped

- 3 cloves garlic, minced

- 1 (16-ounce) jar Alfredo sauce

- 1 cup milk

- 2 cups shredded Havarti cheese

- 1 cup shredded provolone cheese

- 1 cup shredded mozzarella cheese

- 3/4 cup grated Parmesan cheese, divided

- 1 (16-ounce) package frozen fully cooked meatballs, thawed

Steps to Make It

1. Gather the **Ingredients**.

2. Preheat the oven to 375 F. Spray a 9-by-13-inch glass baking dish with nonstick baking spray containing flour and set aside.

3. Bring a large pot of salted water to a boil. Add the penne to the water and cook according to the package directions.

4. Meanwhile, in a large saucepan, melt the butter over medium heat. Add the onion and garlic and cook until tender, about 5 to 7 minutes.

5. When the pasta is done, drain well and set aside.

6. Add the Alfredo sauce and milk to the onion mixture and heat until steaming.

7. Add the Havarti, provolone, mozzarella, and 1/2 cup Parmesan cheese to this mixture and cook over low heat until cheese melts.

8. Stir in drained pasta and the meatballs.

9. Pour the mixture into the prepared dish. Top with the remaining 1/4 cup Parmesan cheese.

10. Bake for 25 to 30 minutes or until the casserole is bubbly around the edges and the cheese starts to brown on top.

11. Serve and enjoy!

Tip

• To make ahead of time, do not bake; cover and refrigerate up to 24 hours, or freeze up to one month. Bake chilled casserole for an additional 10 to 15 minutes. Thaw the frozen casserole in the fridge overnight, then bake until hot and bubbly.

Chicken Burgers

Ingredients

- For the Chicken Burgers:

- 2 to 3 teaspoons vegetable oil

- 1/3 cup finely chopped onion

- 2 medium cloves garlic (finely minced)

- 1 to 1 1/4 pounds boneless chicken thighs

- 1 cup loosely packed cilantro or parsley, or a combination

- 1 tablespoon freshly squeezed lime juice

- 1/2 teaspoon Cajun seasoning

- 1/2 teaspoon salt

- 1/4 teaspoon freshly ground black pepper

- 1/4 cup fine dry breadcrumbs

- 1 egg white

- For Burger Assembly:

- 6 to 8 hamburger rolls (toasted)

- Burger toppings such as lettuce, tomato, and onion

- Condiments such as ketchup, mayonnaise, and mustard

Steps to Make It

1. Gather the **Ingredients**.

2. Preheat the oven to 400 F. Line a baking sheet with aluminum foil or spray with nonstick baking spray.

3. In a small skillet, heat the oil over medium heat. Add the minced onion and cook, stirring, until tender. Add the garlic and cook, stirring, for another 1 to 2 minutes. Remove from the heat and set aside.

4. Cut the chicken into chunks, discarding excess fat. Grind with a meat grinder or mince finely in the food processor. Add the herb, lime juice, seasonings, breadcrumbs, and the onion and garlic mixture. Mix until combined.

5. Chop the cilantro or parsley finely and mix into the chicken mixture.

6. Shape the chicken mixture into patties about 3 to 4 ounces each and place on the baking sheet.

7. Bake for about 20 minutes, or until cooked through.

8. Serve these flavorful chicken burgers on split toasted hamburger rolls with your favorite burger toppings.

Instant Pot Sloppy Joes Recipe

Ingredients

- 1 tablespoon vegetable oil

- 2 pounds ground beef, 85 percent or leaner

- 1 1/2 cups onion, chopped

- 1 cup green bell pepper, chopped

- 1 clove garlic, minced

- 2/3 cup water

- 2 cups ketchup

- 3 tablespoons brown sugar

- 1 1/2 tablespoons Worcestershire sauce

- 1 tablespoon Dijon mustard

- 8 sandwich buns

Steps to Make It

1. Gather the **Ingredients**.

2. Select the Instant Pot's sauté setting and add the oil. When the oil is hot and shimmering, add the ground beef. Cook for 4 minutes, stirring constantly.

3. Add the onion, bell pepper, and garlic to the beef and cook for 2 to 3 minutes longer, stirring frequently.

4. Add the water to the pot and stir, scraping the bottom of the pot to loosen any stuck-on browned bits.

5. In a bowl, combine the ketchup, brown sugar, Worcestershire sauce, and mustard. Add the mixture to the Instant Pot; do not stir.

6. Lock the lid in place and turn the steam release knob to the sealing position. Choose the pressure cook or manual setting (high pressure) and set the timer for 10 minutes. When the time is up, let the pressure come down naturally for 10 minutes and then carefully do a quick release following the manufacturer's instructions.

7. Cancel the pressure cook function and choose the sauté button. Continue cooking the sloppy joe mixture for 2 to 3 minutes, or until reduced and thickened.

8. Spoon the sloppy joe sauce over toasted buns and serve with chips, fries, or tater tots.

Potato Chip Chicken Recipe

Ingredients

• 4 chicken breasts

• 1 (5-ounce) bag barbecue potato chips

• 1 cup all- purpose flour

• 1 teaspoon garlic powder

• 1 teaspoon salt

- 1 teaspoon freshly ground black pepper

- 2 large eggs

Steps to Make It

1. Gather the **Ingredients**.

2. Split the chicken breasts in half, so that you have 2 thinner cutlets. Preheat the oven to 400 F.

3. Pound each breast until they are around a quarter-inch thick.

4. Place the potato chips in a plastic bag and press out all of the air. Use a rolling pin to crush the potato chips. Place them in a shallow bowl until you are ready to dip them.

5. Season the flour with the garlic powder, salt, and pepper. Whisk to evenly distribute the spices. Dip

the chicken into the flour mixture and coat both sides.

6. Whisk the eggs until very well beaten. Dip the chicken into the egg mixture and coat on both sides.

7. Place the chicken into the potato chips and press the chips all over the chicken on both sides.

8. Put a cooling rack on top of a baking sheet. Place the chicken onto the rack. You may need two baking sheets to fit all of the chicken.

9. Place the chicken in the oven and bake for about twenty minutes or until crunchy and cooked through. In the summer, serve with a fresh salad and dipping sauce. Or serve with rice or mashed

potatoes and a steamed vegetable in colder weather.

Tip

• Place the chicken in a plastic bag or between two sheets of plastic wrap while you are pounding them to avoid a mess.

Easy Chicken Parmesan

Ingredients

• 4 boneless chicken breasts, about 1 1/2 pounds

• 1 large egg

• 1/2 cup milk

• 1/2 cup seasoned breadcrumbs, preferably Italian flavored

- Olive oil

- 8 slices low-moisture mozzarella cheese

- 1 (24-ounce) jar pasta sauce

- 1/2 cup grated Parmesan cheese

- 8 ounces spaghetti, or linguine

Steps to Make It

1. Gather the **Ingredients**.

2. Lightly grease a 9x13-inch baking dish. Heat the oven to 350 F.

3. Put the chicken breasts between sheets of plastic wrap and gently pound to about 1/2 inch in thickness. Use a rolling pin or the flat side of a meat mallet.

4. In a medium bowl, whisk together the egg and milk.

5. Place the seasoned breadcrumbs in a different wide and shallow bowl.

6. Dip the flattened chicken breasts in the milk and egg mixture and then in the seasoned breadcrumbs, turning each piece to coat it evenly.

7. In a large skillet or sauté pan heat 1 inch of olive oil over medium heat until hot (if you dip a corner of a breaded chicken breast in the oil it should sizzle briskly). Be careful not to burn it, as olive oil achieves the smoke point fairly fast.

8. Brown the chicken in the hot oil on both sides until golden brown, 3 to 4 minutes per side.

9. Pour 1/3 of the pasta sauce on the bottom of the prepared baking dish. Place the chicken on top and use 7 mozzarella slices to cover the chicken.

10. Pour the remaining sauce over the chicken and cheese. Sprinkle Parmesan cheese on top. Tear the remaining mozzarella slice into pieces and scatter on top. Bake for 25 to 30 minutes, or until bubbly.

11. While the chicken bakes, cook the spaghetti or linguine in boiling salted water following package directions. Drain well.

12. Serve the chicken with the pasta, bread, and a tossed green salad.

Chinese Orange Pork Chop Stir-Fry

Ingredients

- 4 boneless pork chops, about 1 1/2 pounds

For Marinade:

- 1 tablespoon rice wine, or dry sherry

- 2 teaspoons cornstarch

For Sauce:

- 1/3 cup orange juice

- 2 tablespoons water

- 2 tablespoons soy sauce

- 1 1/2 teaspoons honey

Other:

- 2 slices ginger, chopped

- 1 clove garlic, chopped

- 2 baby bok choy

- 1/2 cup baby carrots

- 2 teaspoons cornstarch, mixed with 4 teaspoons water

- A few drops sesame oil, as needed

- 4 tablespoons oil, for stir-frying, or as needed

Steps to Make It

1. Gather the **Ingredients**.

2. Cut the pork chops into 1-inch cubes.

3. Add the rice wine and cornstarch and marinate for 30 minutes.

4. While the pork is marinating, prepare the vegetables and sauce. Wash the baby bok choy,

drain, and chop, separating the leaves and the stalks.

5. Cut baby carrots in half.

6. Combine sauce **Ingredients** in a small bowl, set aside. Combine the cornstarch and water in a small bowl and set aside.

7. Heat a wok or heavy gauge frying pan. Add 2 tablespoons oil. When the oil is hot, add the pork chop cubes. Let the pork chops cook for a minute, and then stir-fry until they change color and are nearly cooked. Remove from the wok or pan and drain on paper towels.

8. Clean out the wok and add more oil. When the oil is hot, add the garlic and ginger. Stir-fry briefly until aromatic. Add the carrots. Stir-fry briefly.

9. Add the baby bok choy stalks. Cook briefly, add the leaves and stir-fry briefly until they turn bright green.

10. Make a well in the middle of the wok and add the sauce.

11. Turn up the heat, give the cornstarch and water mixture a quick re-stir, and add it to the sauce, stirring quickly to thicken. Mix everything together.

12. Add a few drops of sesame oil and serve hot. Serve with cooked rice.

Chicken and Stuffing Bake Recipe

Ingredients

- 1/4 cup olive oil

- 2 stalks celery, finely diced

- 1 small onion, diced

- 2 cloves garlic, minced

- 2 pounds boneless, skinless chicken breasts

- 1 teaspoon salt

- 1 teaspoon freshly ground black pepper

- 2 (10 3/4-ounce) cans cream of chicken soup

- 1/4 cup milk

- 1 (6-ounce) box chicken stuffing mix

- 1 1/2 cups chicken broth

- Fresh sage, for garnish, optional

- Parsley, for garnish, optional

Steps to Make It

1. Gather the **Ingredients**.

2. Heat the olive oil in a sauté pan on medium heat. Add the celery, onion, and garlic to the pan and sauté for 3 to 5 minutes or until the vegetables are softened and the onion is translucent. Remove from the heat and set aside.

3. Preheat the oven to 375 F.

4. Cut the chicken breasts into 1-inch pieces. Spray the bottom of a 9 x 13-inch baking dish with nonstick spray. Sprinkle the top of the chicken with the salt and pepper.

5. In a medium bowl whisk together the cream of chicken soup, milk, and cooked vegetable mixture.

6. Pour the mixture over the top of the chicken, covering it completely.

7. Sprinkle the stuffing mix over the top of the chicken. Pour the chicken broth evenly over the stuffing mix. Cover the dish with foil and place it in the oven. Bake the casserole for 40 to 45 minutes, or until the chicken is completely cooked through. The edges will be bubbly.

8. Remove the foil and turn up the heat to 425 F. Place the casserole back in the oven and brown the top for about 5 minutes. Allow the casserole to sit on the counter for about 10 minutes before serving.

9. Sprinkle the top with chopped sage and parsley if desired.

Stuffed Peppers With Ground Beef and Rice

Ingredients

• 6 green bell peppers (or choose a combination of colors)

• 1 tablespoon extra-virgin olive oil

• 1 tablespoon unsalted butter

• 1/2 cup chopped onion

• 1/2 cup chopped celery

• 1 (14.5-ounce) can diced tomatoes

• 1 (8-ounce) can tomato sauce

• 1 clove garlic, crushed and minced

• 1 teaspoon dried oregano

- 1/2 teaspoon dried basil

- 2 teaspoons kosher salt, divided

- 1/2 teaspoon ground black pepper, divided

- 1 large egg, lightly beaten

- 1 1/2 teaspoons Worcestershire sauce

- 1 1/2 pounds lean ground beef (90/10)

- 1 1/2 cups cooked long-grain rice

- Shredded mild cheddar cheese (about 1/2 to 3/4 cup), optional

Steps to Make It

1. Gather the **Ingredients**.

2. Cut the tops off of the bell peppers and rinse them under cold water; remove seeds and cut away the white ribs, which might be bitter. Chop the edible part of tops and set aside. Place the peppers in a large pot and cover with salted water.

3. Bring to a boil. Reduce heat, cover, and simmer for 5 minutes. Drain and set aside.

4. Heat the olive oil and butter in a large skillet over medium heat until oil is hot and the butter is foamy. Sauté the chopped bell pepper (from the tops), chopped onion, and chopped celery for about 5 minutes, or until vegetables are tender.

5. Add the (undrained) canned diced tomatoes, tomato sauce, crushed garlic, oregano, basil, 1 teaspoon salt, and 1/4 teaspoon pepper. Bring to a simmer and cook for about 10 minutes.

6. In a large mixing bowl, combine the egg with the remaining 1 teaspoon of salt, 1/4 teaspoon pepper, and Worcestershire sauce. Gently stir to blend; add ground beef, cooked rice, and 1 cup of the tomato sauce mixture. Mix well.

7. Heat the oven to 350 F.

8. Stuff the peppers loosely with the ground beef mixture and place them in a 13 x 9 x 2-inch baking pan. Pour the remaining tomato mixture over the stuffed peppers.

9. Bake the peppers for about 45 minutes, or until the meat mixture is thoroughly cooked.

Tips

• To ensure the peppers are thoroughly cooked, insert an instant-read thermometer into the center of a stuffed pepper. The minimum safe temperature is 160 F for ground beef, pork, or lamb, or 165 F for ground turkey or chicken.

• Use a baking dish that can accommodate peppers that are closely packed together peppers because they will soften a bit as they cook. You don't want to lose all that hard work with peppers that have fallen over.

• The peppers may also be halved horizontally so you have two halves to fill. You won't have the extra chopped pepper from the tops, but you can chop an extra bell pepper.

Chapter 6: Recommended Kid-Friendly Salad and Side Dish Recipes

Orange Glazed Carrots

Ingredients

4 cups fresh carrots, sliced

1 tsp. margarine

3/4 cup water

3 Tbsp. orange juice concentrate, undiluted

1 Tbsp. cornstarch

1/4 tsp. salt

1/8 tsp. pepper

Cinnamon to taste

Directions

Cook carrots in 3/4 cup water with margarine 10–15 minutes or until tender. Drain cooking water into a measuring cup. Add the juice concentrate and more water to make a total of 1-1/4 cups liquid. Add corn starch and blend well. Pour liquid over carrots in saucepan and cook over low heat stirring frequently until sauce thickens. Season with salt, pepper and cinnamon to taste. Makes 8 1/2 cup servings.

1 serving = 1 vegetable exchange or 5 grams of carbohydrate

Marinated Mushrooms

Ingredients

8 ounces button mushrooms, canned

2 cloves of garlic, halved

1 Tbsp. olive oil

4 tsp. wine vinegar

1/8 tsp. salt

1 dash Tabasco sauce

Directions

Drain mushrooms and reserve liquid. Place mushrooms in glass jar. Mix all other Ingredients and pour over mushrooms. Add enough of the original liquid from the mushrooms to cover them. Shake jar to mix well and refrigerate. Allow mushrooms to marinate 24 hours before serving. Drain and discard liquid from mushrooms. Place a toothpick into each mushroom and arrange on a plate to serve. Makes 4 1/4 cup servings.

1 serving = 1 vegetable or 5 grams of carbohydrates

Stuffed Potatoes

Ingredients

2 Tbsp. olive oil

2 cloves garlic, minced

1 bunch scallions, cut into 2? pieces

6 ounces baby carrots

6 ounces summer squash

6 ounces baby zucchini

6 ounces baby corn

1 cup chicken broth or bouillon

2 cups cherry tomatoes, halved

2 Tbsp. chopped fresh chives

4 medium potatoes, baked

1 cup cheddar cheese, made with 2% milk

Directions

Heat oil on medium in a large skillet. Saute garlic 3 minutes until soft, but not brown. Add vegetables, except tomatoes, and stir-fry 5 minutes until golden brown. Add broth and simmer for about 5 minutes until tender. Add tomatoes and simmer 1 minute. Add chives to taste. Make a horizontal slice in top of each baked potato and spoon vegetable mixture into potato. Add 1/4 cup shredded cheddar cheese to top. Makes 4 servings.

1 serving = 3 starch + 2 vegetable + 1 meat + 2 fat exchanges or 57 grams of carbohydrate

Scalloped Potatoes

Ingredients

2 cups potatoes, thinly sliced

1/2 cup mushrooms, sliced

1/2 cup onions, sliced

4 beef bouillon cubes

1-1/2 cups boiling water

1 tsp. butter flavored salt

Pinch of pepper

Pinch of nutmeg

Instructions

Preheat oven to 350 degrees. Mix potatoes, mushrooms and onions in non-stick baking dish. Dissolve bouillon cubes in water, blend in salt, pepper and nutmeg; pour over vegetables. Cover and bake for 45 minutes. Uncover and bake an additional 15–20 minutes. Makes four serving of 3/4 cup each.

1 serving = 1 starch exchange or 17 grams of carbohydrate

Nutty Broccoli

Ingredients

2/3 cup brazil nuts, thinly sliced

1/2 cup bread crumbs

1 Tbsp. lemon juice

3 Tbsp. margarine

1 tsp. salt

3 pounds fresh broccoli, cut in spears

1/4 cup margarine, melted

1 Tbsp. lemon juice

Instructions

Melt the 3 tablespoons of margarine in a large frying pan. Add 1 Tbsp. lemon juice, nuts and bread crumbs. Cook until bread crumbs and nuts are toasted. Bring 1 inch of water to boil in large saucepan. Add salt and broccoli. Cover and simmer 12 minutes or until broccoli is semi-tender. Drain. Mix together 1/4 cup margarine and 1 tablespoon lemon juice. Arrange broccoli on platter with flower of broccoli along outside of platter. Drizzle with margarine mixture. Sprinkle stems with bread crumb mixture and serve. Makes 12 servings.

1 serving = 2 vegetable + 2 fat exchanges or 8 grams of carbohydrates

Superfood Chopped Salad with Salmon & Creamy Garlic Dressing

Ingredients

- 1 pound salmon fillet

- ½ cup low-fat plain yogurt

- ¼ cup mayonnaise

- 2 tablespoons lemon juice

- 2 tablespoons grated Parmesan cheese

- 1 tablespoon finely chopped fresh parsley

- 1 tablespoon snipped fresh chives

- 2 teaspoons reduced-sodium tamari or soy sauce

- 1 medium clove garlic, minced

- ¼ teaspoon ground pepper

- 8 cups chopped curly kale

- 2 cups chopped broccoli

- 2 cups chopped red cabbage

- 2 cups finely diced carrots

- ½ cup sunflower seeds, toasted

Directions

1. Arrange rack in upper third of oven. Preheat broiler to high. Line a baking sheet with foil.

2. Place salmon on the prepared baking sheet, skin-side down. Broil, rotating the pan from front to back once, until the salmon is opaque in the center, 8 to 12 minutes. Cut into 4 portions.

3. Meanwhile, whisk yogurt, mayonnaise, lemon juice, Parmesan, parsley, chives, tamari (or soy sauce), garlic and pepper in a small bowl.

4. Combine kale, broccoli, cabbage, carrots and sunflower seeds in a large bowl. Add 3/4 cup of the dressing and toss to coat. Divide the salad among 4 dinner plates and top each with a piece of salmon and about 1 tablespoon of the remaining dressing.

High-Protein Grilled Chicken Salad

Ingredients

- 1 small red onion

- 5 tablespoons red-wine vinegar, divided

- 2 medium cloves garlic, grated

- 1 teaspoon Dijon mustard

- 1 ½ teaspoons salt, divided

- ⅔ cup grapeseed oil, plus more for grill grates

- ½ teaspoon paprika

- 1 medium zucchini, sliced lengthwise into 1/2-inch-thick planks

- 1 small yellow bell pepper, cut into 2-inch-thick strips

- 2 large romaine lettuce hearts, halved lengthwise

- 3 (8 ounce) boneless, skinless chicken breasts

- 1 (5 ounce) package fresh baby spinach

- 2 small tomatoes, cut into 1-inch wedges

Directions

1. Preheat grill to medium-high (400°F to 450°F). Halve onion lengthwise through root end. Cut 1 half into 1-inch wedges; set aside. Thinly slice the other half. Place the onion slices in a small bowl; add 2 tablespoons vinegar; toss to combine. Set aside to pickle, stirring occasionally, until ready to use. Drain before serving.

2. Whisk garlic, mustard, 1 teaspoon salt and the remaining 3 tablespoons vinegar together in a large bowl until the salt dissolves. Slowly drizzle in oil, whisking constantly, until the dressing is creamy. Set aside 1/4 cup dressing. Stir paprika into the remaining dressing in the bowl. Combine zucchini slices, bell pepper strips, romaine halves and the reserved onion wedges on a large rimmed baking sheet. Drizzle with 1/2 cup dressing; toss to

coat well, making sure to get dressing between the lettuce leaves. Place chicken in the large bowl with the remaining dressing; toss to coat. Sprinkle with the remaining 1/2 teaspoon salt.

3. Oil the grill grates by holding an oil-soaked paper towel with tongs. Grill the chicken and the vegetables, uncovered, for 1 minute. Continue grilling until the romaine is slightly wilted, about 1 minute more; transfer the romaine to the baking sheet. Continue grilling the chicken and vegetables, covered and turning occasionally, until the vegetables are tender-crisp with grill marks and a thermometer inserted into the thickest portion of chicken registers 165°F, about 6 minutes for the vegetables and 8 to 10 minutes for the chicken. Return the grilled chicken and vegetables to the baking sheet with the romaine; let the

chicken rest for 5 minutes before slicing. Cut the romaine and vegetables into 1-inch chunks.

4. Transfer the chopped romaine to a large bowl. Add spinach and the reserved 1/4 cup dressing; toss well. Arrange the mixture on a large platter; top with sliced chicken, zucchini, bell pepper, tomatoes and pickled onions. Serve immediately.

Fiber-Packed Spicy White Bean & Spinach Salad

Ingredients

• 2 (15-ounce) cans no-salt-added cannellini beans, rinsed

• ⅓ cup whole-milk plain yogurt

• ¾ teaspoon ras el hanout

- ½ teaspoon refrigerated garlic paste

- ½ teaspoon salt

- ½ teaspoon honey

- 2 tablespoons extra-virgin olive oil

- 1 tablespoon red-wine vinegar

- 1 tablespoon harissa paste

- 1 (5 ounce) package baby spinach

- 1 cup julienned carrots

- ¼ cup unsalted roasted almonds, chopped

- 3 tablespoons golden raisins

Directions

1. Combine beans, yogurt, ras el hanout, garlic paste, salt and honey in a medium bowl; stir to incorporate, coarsely mashing beans, if desired.

2. Whisk oil, vinegar and harissa together in a large bowl. Add spinach, carrots, almonds and raisins; toss to coat. Serve the spinach mixture with the bean salad.

Arugula Salad with Roasted Pork Tenderloin, Pears & Blue Cheese

Ingredients

- 2 tablespoons chopped walnuts

- 3 tablespoons balsamic vinegar

- 2 tablespoons extra-virgin olive oil

- 2 teaspoons lemon juice

- 1 teaspoon honey

- 1 teaspoon Dijon mustard

- 2 teaspoons finely chopped fresh rosemary or 3/4 teaspoon dried

- 1 clove garlic, minced

- ½ teaspoon salt, divided

- ½ teaspoon ground pepper, divided

- 1 pound pork tenderloin

- 8 cups arugula

- 4 small or 2 large red pears, sliced into wedges

- ¼ cup crumbled blue cheese

Directions

1. Preheat oven to 400 degrees F. Coat a large rimmed baking sheet with cooking spray.

2. Cook walnuts in a medium skillet over medium heat, stirring frequently, until golden and fragrant. Set aside.

3. Whisk vinegar, oil, lemon juice, honey, mustard, rosemary, garlic, and 1/4 teaspoon each salt and pepper in a large bowl. Place pork on the prepared baking sheet. Brush with 1 tablespoon of the dressing and sprinkle with the remaining 1/4 teaspoon each salt and pepper.

4. Roast the pork until a thermometer registers 145 degrees F, 20 to 22 minutes. Transfer to a clean

cutting board and let stand for 5 minutes. Cut into slices about 3/4 inch thick.

5. Add arugula and pears to the dressing in the large bowl and toss to coat. Divide the salad among 4 serving plates. Top with pork, cheese, and the reserved walnuts.

Roasted Cabbage Salad with Lemon-Garlic Vinaigrette

Ingredients

• Olive oil cooking spray

• 1 medium head cabbage

• 1/2 teaspoon salt, divided

• Ground pepper to taste

- 1/4 cup extra-virgin olive oil

- 1 1/2 tablespoons red-wine vinegar

- 1 tablespoon lemon juice

- 1 1/2 teaspoons Dijon mustard

- 1 small clove garlic, grated

- 2 tablespoons sliced almonds, toasted (see Tip)

- 2 tablespoons minced fresh chives or parsley

Directions

1. Preheat oven to 400°F. Line a large rimmed baking sheet with foil, parchment paper or a silicone baking mat; coat lightly with olive oil cooking spray.

2. Remove any damaged outer leaves from cabbage and cut into 8 wedges, keeping the core intact to hold them together. Arrange the wedges on the prepared pan. Coat the tops of the wedges lightly with cooking spray and season with ¼ teaspoon salt and pepper to taste.

3. Roast the cabbage, rotating the pan from back to front and flipping the wedges halfway, until tender and golden, 30 to 40 minutes.

4. Meanwhile, combine oil, vinegar, lemon juice, mustard, garlic, the remaining ¼ teaspoon salt and pepper to taste in a jar with a tight-fitting lid. Cover and shake until well blended.

5. Let the cabbage cool for 5 minutes, then coarsely chop. Transfer to a shallow serving dish and

drizzle with the dressing. Sprinkle with almonds and chives (or parsley) before serving.

Padma Lakshmi's Tandoori Chicken Salad

Ingredients

Chicken

- 1 cup nonfat plain yogurt

- 2 teaspoons garam masala

- 1 teaspoon ground ginger

- 1 teaspoon minced garlic

- 1 teaspoon ground turmeric

- 1 teaspoon salt

- 1 jalapeño pepper, stemmed, seeded and finely minced (optional)

- 1 ½ pounds boneless, skinless chicken breasts, gently flattened and cut into 1/2-inch strips

- 1 tablespoon canola oil

Salad

- 3 cups shredded iceberg lettuce

- 3 cups shredded red cabbage

- 3 cups diced plum tomatoes

- 2 cups sliced cucumber

- 1 ½ cups diced jicama

- 1 cup sliced radishes

• 1 small bunch scallions, finely chopped

• 1 cup loosely packed cilantro leaves, finely chopped

• Juice of 2 small lemons, or to taste

Directions

1. To make chicken: Whisk yogurt, garam masala, ginger, garlic, turmeric, salt and jalapeño (if using) in a shallow dish. Add chicken and stir to coat. Cover and refrigerate while preparing the vegetables.

2. Meanwhile, make salad: Combine lettuce, cabbage, tomatoes, cucumber, jicama, radishes, scallions and cilantro in a large bowl; toss to combine.

3. Heat oil in a large nonstick skillet over medium-high heat. Add the chicken and marinade; cook, stirring occasionally, until an instant-read thermometer inserted in the thickest part registers 165°F, 6 to 8 minutes.

4. Transfer the chicken and the pan juices to the bowl with the salad. Add lemon juice to taste; toss to combine.

Spicy Black-Eyed Pea & Collard Green Salad

Ingredients

• 1 tablespoon neutral oil, such as grapeseed or canola

• 1 small shallot, chopped

• 1 clove garlic, thinly sliced

- ½ cup finely chopped yellow and/or red bell pepper

- 1 cup thinly sliced collard greens, coarsely chopped

- ½ teaspoon harissa paste (see Note)

- ¼ - ½ teaspoon peri-peri sauce (see Note)

- 2 cups cooked black-eyed peas or 1 15-ounce can no-salt-added black-eyed peas, rinsed

- ½ teaspoon turbinado sugar

- ¼ teaspoon sea salt

- ⅛ teaspoon ground pepper

- ¼ cup roughly chopped stemmed flat-leaf parsley

- 3 tablespoons extra-virgin olive oil

- 1 tablespoon lemon juice

- 1 tablespoon finely chopped preserved lemon

- 1 medium tomato, chopped

Directions

1. Heat neutral oil in a medium skillet over medium heat. Add shallot and garlic; cook, stirring, until fragrant and slightly golden, 1 to 2 minutes. Add bell pepper; cook, stirring occasionally, until starting to soften, 1 to 3 minutes. Add collard greens; cook, stirring, until slightly wilted, 1 to 2 minutes. Stir in harissa and peri-peri sauce, then mix in black-eyed peas. Season with sugar, salt and pepper. Reduce heat to

low; cook, stirring occasionally, 3 to 5 minutes. Taste and adjust seasoning, if desired.

2. Transfer the mixture to a medium bowl. Add parsley, olive oil, lemon juice and preserved lemon; mix well. Fold in tomato and adjust seasoning, if desired.

Green Goddess Tuna Salad

Ingredients

• 1 large clove garlic, peeled

• 1/2 medium shallot, peeled

• 1 cup fresh herbs with tender stems, such as dill, cilantro, basil, parsley and/or chives, plus more for garnish

- 1/2 cup lemon juice or lime juice

- 1/4 cup extra-virgin olive oil

- 1/4 cup whole-milk plain strained yogurt, such as Greek-style

- 1/2 teaspoon salt

- 1/4 teaspoon honey

- 1/8 teaspoon ground pepper or crushed red pepper, plus more for garnish

- 2 (5-oz.) cans no-salt-added water-packed tuna, drained

Directions

1. Place garlic in a food processor; pulse until chopped, about 5 seconds. Add shallot; pulse until

chopped, about 5 seconds. Add herbs, lemon (or lime) juice, oil, yogurt, salt, honey and pepper (or crushed red pepper); process until totally combined and smooth, about 1 minute, scraping down sides as needed.

2. Place tuna in a medium bowl and gently flake with a fork. Pour half of the dressing (about 1/3 cup) over the tuna; stir to combine. (Reserve the remaining dressing for another use.) Garnish with herbs and pepper, if desired.

Seafood Salad

Ingredients

- 3 lemons, divided

- ⅔ cup extra-virgin olive oil

- ½ cup chopped fresh flat-leaf parsley

- 2 teaspoons chopped fresh oregano

- 2 cloves garlic, grated

- ½ teaspoon salt

- ½ teaspoon crushed red pepper

- 2 tablespoons white vinegar plus 1/2 cup, divided

- 1 fennel bulb, cored and very thinly sliced

- 1 cup thinly sliced red onion

- 16 cups water

- 1 pound peeled and deveined medium shrimp

- 1 pound large scallops

- ½ pound squid (tubes), cleaned and sliced into 1/4-inch rings

- 1 (4.2-ounce) can smoked mussels in olive oil, drained

Directions

1. Zest and juice 2 lemons into a large shallow bowl; cut the remaining lemon into 1/4-inch rounds and set aside. Add oil, parsley, oregano, garlic, salt, crushed red pepper and 2 tablespoons vinegar to the shallow bowl; whisk vigorously until the mixture looks creamy, about 30 seconds. Add fennel and onion to the bowl; stir gently and set aside.

2. Combine 16 cups water, the remaining 1/2 cup vinegar and the reserved lemon rounds in a large

stockpot; bring to a boil over high heat. Fill a large bowl with ice water; place near the stove. Add shrimp to the boiling water; cook until opaque and cooked through, about 2 minutes. With a slotted spoon, transfer the shrimp to the ice bath. Return the water to a boil over high heat; add scallops and squid; cook until the scallops are opaque and the squid slices are tender, 1 to 2 minutes. Drain and transfer the scallops and squid to the ice bath. When all the seafood is cool to the touch, pat dry with paper towels and add to the bowl with the dressing. Add mussels and toss to combine.

Tuna Niçoise Salad

Ingredients

- 10 ounces baby yellow or red potatoes (about 2 cups), scrubbed

- 1 cup halved crosswise fresh green beans

- 3 tablespoons fresh lemon juice

- 2 tablespoons finely chopped shallot

- 1 teaspoon Dijon mustard

- ½ teaspoon salt, divided

- ½ teaspoon ground pepper, divided

- 5 tablespoons extra-virgin olive oil, divided

- 1 tablespoon chopped fresh flat-leaf parsley

- 1 (8 ounce) fresh tuna steak

- 8 cups torn green leaf or Bibb lettuce

- 2 hard-boiled eggs, peeled and halved lengthwise

- 1 cup halved cherry tomatoes

- ½ cup pitted Niçoise olives

Directions

1. Place a steamer basket in the bottom of a large pot and add water to just below the bottom of the basket. Cover and bring to a boil over high heat. Add potatoes to the basket and reduce heat to medium; cook, covered, until tender, about 15 minutes. (Do not remove pot from heat.) Transfer potatoes to a plate and let cool for about 10 minutes.

2. Meanwhile, add green beans to the basket; cook over medium heat, covered, until tender-crisp,

about 5 minutes. Transfer the beans to the plate with the potatoes. Cut the cooled potatoes in half crosswise.

3. Whisk lemon juice, shallot, mustard and 1/4 teaspoon each salt and pepper in a medium bowl until smooth. Whisking constantly, gradually drizzle in 4 tablespoons oil. Whisk in parsley until combined.

4. Pat tuna dry; sprinkle with the remaining 1/4 teaspoon each salt and pepper. Heat the remaining 1 tablespoon oil in a medium nonstick skillet over medium heat. Add the tuna and cook, turning once, until lightly browned, about 2 minutes per side. Transfer to a clean cutting board and let rest for 5 minutes. Slice 1/2-inch thick against the grain.

5. Arrange lettuce on a platter or 4 plates; top with the sliced tuna, halved potatoes, green beans, eggs, tomatoes and olives. Drizzle evenly with the dressing and serve immediately.

Cashew, Chickpea & Pasta Salad with Cilantro-Mint-Shallot Vinaigrette

Ingredients

• 2 ounces lentil or whole-grain pasta, such as fusilli or penne

• 1 medium shallot, finely diced

• 1 tablespoon lemon juice

• 1 tablespoon warm water

• ½ teaspoon fine sea salt, divided

- ¼ cup finely chopped fresh cilantro

- ¼ cup finely chopped fresh mint

- 2 tablespoons extra-virgin olive oil

- 1 ½ tablespoons red-wine vinegar

- 1 teaspoon Dijon mustard

- 1 small clove garlic, minced

- ¾ cup no-salt-added chickpeas, rinsed

- ½ medium red bell pepper, cut into 1-inch pieces

- ½ medium yellow bell pepper, cut into 1-inch pieces

- ½ large avocado, diced

- 2 stalks celery, thinly sliced

- ½ cup arugula

- 3 tablespoons unsalted roasted cashews, roughly chopped

Directions

1. Bring a medium pot of water to a boil. Cook pasta according to package Directions, omitting salt. Drain and rinse with cold water.

2. Meanwhile, combine shallot, lemon juice, warm water and 1/4 teaspoon salt in a small bowl. Set aside for 10 minutes.

3. Combine cilantro, mint, oil, vinegar, mustard, garlic and the remaining 1/4 teaspoon salt in a large bowl. Add the shallot mixture, the cooled pasta, chickpeas, red bell pepper, yellow bell

pepper, avocado, celery, arugula and cashews; toss to combine.

Baked Kale Salad with Crispy Quinoa

Ingredients

- 2 ⅔ cups water

- 1 ⅓ cups quinoa

- Cooking spray

- 4 cups sliced red or green cabbage

- 1 large fennel bulb, trimmed and cut into thin wedges, fronds reserved and chopped for garnish

- 4 tablespoons extra-virgin olive oil, divided

- ¾ teaspoon salt, divided

- 8 cups coarsely chopped kale

- ½ teaspoon ground pepper, divided

- 1 teaspoon lemon zest

- 2 tablespoons lemon juice

- 1 teaspoon honey

- 1 medium clove garlic, finely grated

- ¼ cup crumbled feta cheese

- ¼ cup toasted pepitas

Directions

1. Bring water to a boil in a large saucepan. Stir in quinoa; reduce heat to maintain a simmer, cover and cook until the quinoa is tender and the water is absorbed, about 15 minutes. Transfer to a large

rimmed baking sheet, spreading it out as much as possible. Lightly coat with cooking spray.

2. Meanwhile, position racks in upper and lower thirds of oven; preheat to 400°F.

3. Bake the quinoa on the lower rack for 15 minutes. Remove from the oven, stir and coat again with cooking spray. Bake until lightly browned and crisp, about 15 minutes more. Remove from the oven and toss again.

4. Meanwhile, toss cabbage, fennel, 1 tablespoon oil and 1/4 teaspoon salt in a large bowl. Transfer to a second large rimmed baking sheet and roast on the top rack for 15 minutes. Toss kale, 1 tablespoon oil and 1/4 teaspoon each salt and pepper in the large bowl. After the cabbage mixture has roasted for 15 minutes, add the kale to

the pan, carefully stirring it into the rest of the vegetables. Continue roasting until the vegetables are tender, 5 to 7 minutes more.

5. Meanwhile, whisk the remaining 2 tablespoons oil, lemon zest, lemon juice, honey, garlic and the remaining 1/4 teaspoon each salt and pepper together in the large bowl. Add the roasted vegetables and quinoa and toss to coat. Sprinkle with feta and pepitas. Garnish with the reserved fennel fronds, if desired. Serve warm.

Cabbage Caesar Salad

Ingredients

- 3 tablespoons extra-virgin olive oil, divided

- 1 teaspoon garlic powder

- 4 ounces whole-grain country bread, cut into 1/2-inch cubes

- 2 tablespoons lemon juice

- 2 tablespoons mayonnaise

- 1 teaspoon Dijon mustard

- 1 small clove garlic, grated

- 3/4 teaspoon anchovy paste (optional)

- 1/8 teaspoon salt

- Freshly ground pepper to taste

- 6 cups chopped napa cabbage (12 ounces)

- 1/3 cup shaved Parmesan cheese

Directions

1. Preheat oven to 350°F.

2. Stir 1 1/2 tablespoons oil and garlic powder together in a medium bowl. Add bread cubes and toss to coat. Transfer to a large rimmed baking sheet and bake, stirring once, until browned and crisp, 10 to 12 minutes.

3. Meanwhile, whisk lemon juice, the remaining 1 1/2 tablespoons oil, mayonnaise, mustard, garlic, anchovy paste (if using), salt and pepper in a large bowl until well blended. Add cabbage and Parmesan; toss until coated. Serve topped with the croutons.

Classic Niçoise Salad

Ingredients

- 4 ounces small red or white potatoes (about 4), scrubbed and halved

- ½ cup Easy Anchovy Vinaigrette

- 4 ounces fresh green beans (1 cup), trimmed

- ¾ cup rinsed canned chickpeas

- 1 cup cherry or grape tomatoes, halved

- 2 ½ ounces water-packed light tuna, drained

- 2 hard-boiled eggs, quartered

- Chopped fresh parsley for garnish

Directions

1. Bring 1 inch of water to a boil in a large saucepan fitted with a steamer basket. Add potatoes to the basket; cover and steam until tender, 10 to 12

minutes. Transfer the potatoes to a medium bowl. Add vinaigrette and toss gently with a flexible spatula to coat. Let the potatoes stand in the dressing for a minute or two. Using a slotted spoon, transfer the potatoes to a platter or divide between 2 plates.

2. Add green beans to the steamer basket, cover and steam until tender-crisp, 4 to 6 minutes. Rinse under cold running water to stop the cooking.

3. Arrange the green beans, chickpeas, tomatoes, tuna, and eggs on the platter (or plates). Drizzle the remaining dressing from the bowl over the salad. Garnish with parsley, if desired.

Strawberry & Tuna Spinach Salad

Ingredients

- 4 cups baby spinach

- ⅓ cup tuna salad

- ½ cup sliced white mushrooms

- ½ cup strawberries

- ¼ cup sliced red onion

- 2 tablespoons chopped celery

- 1 ½ tablespoons slivered almonds

- 1 tablespoon lemon juice

- ¼ cup mixed fresh fruit

- ¼ cup yogurt

Directions

1. Mix spinach, tuna salad, mushrooms, strawberries, and celery in a medium bowl. Drizzle lemon juice and sprinkle almonds on top.

2. Mix fruit and yogurt in a small bowl. Serve on the side.

Tips

Tip: Spinach is a dark leafy green that provides fiber and a super dose of antioxidant vitamins A, C, and E to support heart health.

Lemony Lentil Salad with Salmon

Ingredients

- ⅓ cup lemon juice

- ⅓ cup chopped fresh dill

- 2 teaspoons Dijon mustard

- ¼ teaspoon salt

- Freshly ground pepper to taste

- ⅓ cup extra-virgin olive oil

- 1 medium red bell pepper, seeded and diced

- 1 cup diced seedless cucumber

- ½ cup finely chopped red onion

- 2 15-ounce cans lentils, rinsed, or 3 cups cooked brown or green lentils (see Tip)

- 2 7-ounce cans salmon, drained and flaked, or 1 1/2 cups flaked cooked salmon

Directions

1. Whisk lemon juice, dill, mustard, salt and pepper in a large bowl. Gradually whisk in oil. Add bell pepper, cucumber, onion, lentils and salmon; toss to coat.

Tips

Make Ahead Tip: Cover and refrigerate for up to 8 hours.

Tip: To cook lentils: Place in a saucepan, cover with water and bring to a boil. Reduce heat to a simmer and cook until just tender, about 20 minutes for green lentils and 30 minutes for brown. Drain and rinse under cold water.

Chapter 7: Final Thought

Following a diabetes treatment plan requires 24-hour care and significant lifestyle changes. Careful management of type 1 diabetes helps reduce your child's risk of serious complications.

As your child gets older:

• Encourage him or her to take an increasingly active role in diabetes management

• Stress the importance of lifelong diabetes care

• Teach your child how to test his or her blood sugar and inject insulin

• Help your child make wise food choices

• Encourage your child to remain physically active

• Foster a relationship between your child and his or her diabetes treatment team

• Make sure your child wears a medical identification tag

The habits you teach your child today will help him or her enjoy an active and healthy life with type 1 diabetes.

School and diabetes

You'll need to work with your child's day care provider or school nurse and teachers to make sure they know the signs and symptoms of high and low blood sugar levels. The school nurse might need to administer insulin or check your child's blood sugar levels.

Federal law protects children with diabetes, and schools must make reasonable accommodations to ensure that all children get a proper education.

Ask your health care provider

Contact your child's health care provider, certified diabetes care and education specialist, or registered dietitian between appointments if you have questions.

Coping and support

If managing your child's diabetes seems overwhelming, take it one day at a time. Some days you'll manage your child's blood sugar ideally and on other days, it may seem as if nothing works well. No one can do it perfectly. But your efforts are worthwhile. Don't forget that you're not alone and that your diabetes treatment team can help.

Your child's emotions

Diabetes can affect your child's emotions both directly and indirectly. Poorly controlled blood sugar can cause behavior changes, such as irritability.

Diabetes can also make your child feel different from other kids. Having to draw blood and give shots sets kids with diabetes apart from their peers. Getting your child together with other children who have diabetes or spending time at a diabetes camp may help your child feel less alone.

Mental health and substance abuse

People with diabetes have an increased risk of depression, anxiety and diabetes-related distress. That's why some diabetes specialists regularly include a social worker or psychologist as part of their diabetes care team.

If you notice that your child or adolescent is persistently sad or pessimistic, or experiences dramatic changes in sleeping habits, weight, friends or school performance, have your child screened for depression.

Rebellion also may be an issue, particularly for teens. A child who has been very good about sticking to his or her diabetes treatment plan may rebel in the teen years by ignoring his or her diabetes care. Additionally, experimenting with drugs, alcohol and smoking can be even more dangerous for people with diabetes.

Support groups

Talking to a counselor or therapist may help your child or you cope with the dramatic lifestyle changes that come with a diagnosis of type 1 diabetes. Your child may find encouragement and understanding in a type 1 diabetes support group for children. Support groups for parents also are available.

If you're interested, your health care provider may be able to recommend a group in your area. Websites that offer support include:

• The American Diabetes Association (ADA). The ADA also offers diabetes camp programs that provide education and support for children and teens with diabetes.

• Juvenile Diabetes Research Foundation (JDRF).

Putting information in perspective

The threat of complications from poorly managed diabetes can be frightening. If you and your child work with your child's health care provider and do your best to manage your child's diabetes, your child will likely live a long and enjoyable life.

Made in the USA
Middletown, DE
11 September 2024